"Be yourself; everyone else is already taken.

— oscar wilde **"**

HOLLYWOOD INTUITION

[It's what separates fashion victims
from fashion victors!]

BY JAYE HERSH
with KAREN SALMANSOHN

 powerHouse Books Brooklyn, NY

Table of contents:

[INTRODUCTION]   6

THE HOLLYWOOD INTUITION
PHILOSOPHY

[PEOPLE]   22

SIRENISTA   26

INGÉNUE   30

YOGANISTA   34

BOHEMIAN PRINCESS   38

ROCK-N-ROLLER   42

FASHIONISTA   46

MIX 'N MATCH   50

[PLACES] 52

STARCUPS RUN 54

PLAYGROUND RUN 58

ACTUAL RUN 62

WEIGHT CENTER RUN 66

FIRST DATE 70

LAST DATE 74

BFF DATE 78

MEETING [WITHOUT A
  CASTING COUCH] 82

PLANES, TRAINS, AND
  LIMOUSINES 86

RED CARPET 90

[THINGS] 94

HATS 96

NECKLACES 97

BAGS 98

RINGS & BLING 100

SCARVES 102

FASHION TAPE 103

SCENTILATIONS 104

BELTS 105

UNDERGARMENTOS 106

GLASSES 108

THE HOLLYWOOD
INTUITION PHILOSOPHY

WHICH WOULD YOU GUESS PEOPLE
ARE MORE FASCINATED WITH: THE RELA-
TIONSHIP LIVES OF CELEBRITIES — OR
THE CLOTHING LIVES OF CELEBRITIES?
It seems to be the latter – if you're judging
by the infinite amount of magazine pages
devoted to who's wearing what – and who's
wearing it best. It's not only interesting to
note how many more pages are devoted
to celebrity style than to celebrity sex,
but also how often a celebrity's sex life can
influence her style life.

For example, I've personally witnessed how
after a famous actress lost her handsome
lover – once spotted with her everywhere
– she quickly gained a gorgeous new Fendi
bag, which rarely left her side. Plus, I've witnessed how soon after a hunk A-list actor –
famously known for draping himself all over
his super-hot-super-famous actress wife –
got a divorce from said wife, this said wife
immediately began draping herself instead

with a gorgeous Hermès scarf – bought in two different colors.

How do I know all this? I'm the go-to stylist for the most sought after A-list celebrities, and the owner of **INTUITION**, the top LA fashion store these actresses migrate to on a regular basis.

I LOVE FASHION and have always had a strong intuition for what the next new trend will be – long before it hits the streets – or movie studios.

My path to becoming a celebrity stylist and celebrity-magnetized store owner is a rather bumpy one. It began after a difficult divorce, which left me veritably bankrupt. I needed cash quickly – so I began selling beautiful cashmere sweaters from the trunk of my car. Thankfully, word spread fast among the Hollywood elite how I had this tremendous intuition about what would become the

next big fashion thing. Not just in cashmere sweaters – but in necklaces, belts, scarves – you name it. And so my business began growing quickly, attracting more and more celebrity clients. Eventually, I became happily able to open up a retail store, in a hidden nook of LA. I named the store "**INTUITION**," because it was my style intuition which saved me from potential homelessness – and paid for my two kids' college tuitions.

It was a tumultuous journey to become a top celeb stylist, Intuition store owner – and now an accessories designer for Target. Indeed, it was a riches-to-rags-to-riches story. Since I fully understand being in the position of wanting fab style without having the BIG budget to afford it, I want to start this book by sharing one of my main style beliefs...

[**Jaye-ism**
You can create the look of fame, without spending a fortune.]

Yes, I VERY personally know what it's like to be low on cash and still want to be wearing high fashion. One of my goals for creating my store, and my line of Target accessories – and now this book – is to help women everywhere develop fabulous celebrity style, without needing to fund it with a celebrity's platinum card.

How can this be? It's simple. Having a terrific sense of style is mostly about confidence, spiritedness, playfulness – an inner joie de vivre! When an actress is emanating star quality, it's not because of all the bling sparkling from her body, but rather how much self-love she has glowing from within. In fact, a true star doesn't need to wear any bling to shine. She could wear jeans, a tee, and a cute necklace – and look like a million. Have you ever looked at someone and thought: "I think that's a celebrity – I just don't know who that person is – but they look famous!" That's their star quality shining through from within! Star quality explains

why the same outfit can create a different result on different women. Basically, star quality is an attitude. Thankfully for those low on cash, having a confident attitude is **FREE TO ALL!** Which brings me to another style philosophy...

[
Jaye-ism
It's not what you wear,
it's how confidently you
wear it.
]

It's funny. Although [STYLE] might seem like it is a superficial subject – all about a woman's surface self – [STYLE] is actually something which goes much deeper. [STYLE] is an expression of a woman's authentic self – her innermost spirit. Think about it. Every time you choose to wear a particular necklace, hat, or scarf, you're making more than a fashion statement – **YOU'RE MAKING A [PERSONAL SPIRIT] STATEMENT ABOUT WHO YOU ARE DEEP INSIDE.** You're revealing a little bit about your personality, values, humor – at

"we convince by our presence.

– walt whitman **"**

times even your politics! For this reason, the more you really know who you are inside of you, the more confidence you have to choose the fashions you wear on the outside of you.

Because I recognize great style is a dynamic duo of knowing WHAT'S IN (when it comes to runway styles), plus knowing WHAT'S INSIDE YOU (when it comes to your attitude/spirit), this book will give you tips in both arenas – both the WHAT'S IN and the WHAT'S INSIDE YOU.

[
Jaye-ism
Fabulous style is a dynamic duo of what's IN and what's INSIDE you.
]

I recognize that as a top celebrity stylist I could easily give you lots of universal style tips. I could tell you that you must "always" wear this or that. But an "always" doesn't really serve anybody. Yes, there are many basic strategies to follow so you look more stylish.

I will be giving you many insider celebrity secrets. But I want to keep reminding you: At the end of the day, every woman must listen to her **INTUITION.**

If you diligently follow my insider celebrity style tips, you will definitely see a change in how you look – to a certain degree. But for real "star quality" makeover results, it's not enough to dress up your body. You must also nurture your mind, heart, and spirit – and allow them to be FULLY EXPRESSED in the fashions you wear. With all this in mind, coming up I will be offering many tips for knowing yourself more [AND LOVING YOURSELF MORE], so you can feel more confident to pick the most exciting clothes and accessories that best express the truest you. Which brings me to another fashion belief...

[
Jaye-ism
The better you know yourself, the better your personal style.
]

A big secret to my success as a celeb stylist is my quick people-reading skills – which verge on speed people-reading. I can swiftly sense who someone is at their core. My strong people-intuition has come in handy when I style my celeb clients. I'm able to take into consideration that aforementioned dynamic duo – both the WHAT'S IN (when it comes to trends), and the WHAT'S INSIDE (when it comes to an actress' authentic being). As a result, I'm able to **select styles that make an A-list actress feel A+**! These results show when this actress struts her stuff down the street or down a red carpet. Which brings me to my important subtitle philosophy for this book...

What separates fashion victims from fashion victors is intuition.

You should **never** be mindlessly buying clothes and accessories just because everyone else is wearing them! If you mindlessly **BUY, BUY, BUY,** then you risk becoming a shopping robot – a "trendoid" – by not tapping into your human intuition about what truly fits you on the inside of you! Instead, you should always be mindfully buying clothes and accessories because they speak to your heart – and your intuition tells you something is **A PERFECT FIT FOR YOU, YOU, YOU.**

I know a lot of women don't trust their **INTUITION** when it comes to fashion – or in a lot of arenas of their life. That's a shame. Learning to trust your intuition will always bring you better life choices, and thereby greater happiness in life.

Many women lack confidence in their intuition, and so they shop in groups. I empathize. I know. We all love feedback. It doesn't matter if you're a girl in need of a friend's support or a celebrity seeking advice from a stylist. We love validation. But I believe the questions we are busy posing to others, should really be posed inwardly. When you can learn to really know and trust yourself – first and foremost – you will find playing around with your personal style is far more fun – because you'll be super fluent in the language of self expression.

With this in mind, in the pages ahead I will be asking you questions which will get you thinking about who you really are – at your core. I know this is unusual for a style book – **to ask you to take a long look inside** – instead of simply asking you to swirl around in front of a mirror. But, hey, this book is not your ordinary style book, because I don't want you to simply have ordinary style. I want you to stand out from the crowd! And to stand out, you cannot follow the herd! Instead you must follow your **INTUITION** and thereby know confidently for yourself which clothes and accessories you should be flaunting.

I've always loved that famous quote: **Give a man a fish, feed him for a day. Teach a man to fish, feed him for life.** Likewise, I recognize it's very easy to give you universal style tips – and thereby dress you for a day – or a week.

I figure if I teach you the basics of style, then go this extra step further and show you how to tap into your intuition about who you really are inside – you can be your own inner-stylist for life. How fantastic is that?

I gotta say, I will feel this book has truly succeeded if when you are done, you can toss it aside and shop with great confidence all by yourself – with only your instincts to keep you company!

In the pages ahead, I will help you build up your style confidence – so you can look at a fashionable something – and just intuitively know if that designer's piece has your name on it! Which brings me to another style philosophy.

> **Jaye-ism**
> **There is no such thing as a piece of clothing or accessory that is a "one-<u>style</u>-fits-all," for all women.**

For example, a leopard print scarf might be a one-SIZE-fits-all – but it's not one-STYLE-fits-all. Sure you can easily slip a leopard print scarf around every single woman's neck – and it will fit. But a leopard print scarf should only be slipped upon a specific type of woman's neck – and it might not be your neck at all!

Think about it. If I recommended that every single woman reading this book runs out to buy a leopard print scarf, I'd be a bad stylist. Meaning? You should be reading all my upcoming style recommendations with a mindfulness to recognize what is most right for you! Hence, why it's so very important that you use the power of your intuition to know what clothes and accessories express your TRUE YOU! Plus, it's why the power of intuition will ultimately prevent you from becoming a fashion victim – and empower you to become a fashion victor instead!

I said it before, and I'll keep saying it throughout this book: A big secret to beauty and style is learning to deeply know and cherish who you are at your core!

I recognize that there are many reasons to buy a pretty necklace or a cool bracelet or a sexy pair of pumps. But my most highly preferred reason to shop will always be **PERSONAL SELF EXPRESSION!**

[14]

I feel it's important to view yourself as a treasured and unique work of art – then view the clothes and accessories you buy as a way to add a frame around you – to highlight your inner fabulousness! And those sexy pumps? Those are a pedestal to showcase the natural wonderfulness which is YOU. All of this brings me to another style philosophy...

Jaye-ism
[**The best way to develop a fabulous style is by feeling fabulous on the inside.**]

I recognize that not all women shop when they're feeling fabulous. Unfortunately, I've seen how many women shop for quite the opposite reason – in hopes of adorning themselves with a show stopper outfit or some shiny accessory which will distract others from seeing who they truly are.

Instead of harnessing fashion for self-expression, these women use fashion to cover up their true selves. Their goal is to hide their insecurities and vulnerabilities behind whatever it is that they're wearing!

I've always found it an interesting irony that the women who come into my store with [the most cocky, full-of-themselves, holier-than-thou attitudes], are the ones who wind up being the least confident – needing the most coddling and advice.

I've also witnessed how for many of the Hollywood elite, shopping isn't so much a fun outing, as it is a competitive mission to amass the most status symbols. Many of the Hollywood elite buy things simply because they want what others cannot have. If there is a limited edition bag, they single-mindedly want to make sure they possess this bag.

It's not because they love the bag, but because they love the feeling of beating out other women and owning the bag first. Once this bag is snagged, these women will often only wear it once, then never want to be seen with it again.

One of my favorite stories is how I began a run on the Jelly Kelly handbags. I started a phone tree and made sure everyone knew they were the only one that got the call. All the ladies were given a different time to pick up their bags. They all thought they were the only ones in town to be the first to buy it. Slowly but surely a friend told a friend – who then told a friend. Ultimately friends of friends were begging me to be able to get them this bag.

WHAT I LOVE ABOUT THIS STORY: I love that friends were sharing this fashion find with friends – and that there was a true passion and excitement amidst many of these women when they finally got to fondle and carry this hard-to-get, treasured bag!

WHAT I DON'T LOVE ABOUT THIS STORY: I feel many of the women who bought this bag didn't shop with their hearts – but with their egos. They thereby didn't really attain true pleasure and appreciation from their purchase – which makes me feel – well, in a word – sad.

Once again, my favorite reason to buy a cool hat, or sexy scarf is the PLEASURE OF PERSONAL SELF EXPRESSION.

I want this book to consistently serve as a reminder that when you shop, you should shop with the right lens – by looking for objects of fashion which appeal to your heart!

You know how a true wine lover will sip their wine slowly, mindfully appreciating the wine's color, aroma, and various notes? A true wine lover doesn't slug back the entire bottle in ten minutes – or buy the bottle, take a quick sip, then toss it into the refrigerator or trash.

Similarly, a true "style" lover should mindfully enjoy all the sensory pleasures and delights of their fashion purchase! A true "style" lover should not shop to drown their sorrows or fill an inner void. They should shop to nourish their spirit and express their inner voice.

I recognize this is not what motivates a lot of women to go shopping. Hey, I'm not living in a cave – or a walk-in closet. I'm living here in the real world – or rather in a surreal world – because, after all, I'm living in Hollywood!

I fully know what "real world" and "surreal world" fashion shopping is all about. And I recognize that shopping represents different things to different people. You've heard of shopping lists. Now here's a REASONS FOR SHOPPING LIST...

1. Some women wait until their favorite handbag, shoes, sweater etc. has frayed to nothing before they even begin to shop for a replacement.

2. Some women use shopping to help them feel more important – by gathering an abundance of stuff around them at all times. It makes them feel powerful to amass lots of things. It helps fill up the holes.

3. Some women shop to get revenge on an ex that is still paying the bills – and so they will hoard as much as they can.

4. Some women shop to escape from reality.

5. Some women shop as a quickie mood pick-me-up, or as another form of antidepressant for more serious unhappiness issues.

6. Some women shop because they truly need a specific something as a staple to fill out their wardrobe.

7. Some women shop because they need something fun and wonderful for a special occasion, meeting, event, party, or date.

8. Some women shop to reward themselves for a wonderful feat they've accomplished.

9. Some women shop because they love the feeling of self-expression they derive from wearing a treasured fashion find!

Obviously, I am a big fan of the last few reasons — numbers 6, 7, 8, and 9! I'd love to encourage you to keep these last few reasons in mind as your main inspirations for shopping. Indeed, I want this book to serve as a reminder to enjoy the whole fun and playfulness of dressing up in fabulous clothes and donning fabulous accessories! The best place to start this enjoyment? You must make sure you feel fabulous within!

A huge part of the art of dressing glamorously, is to feel glamorous from the get-go! You must feel as if the world is your movie and you are the star of your life story. Hence, you need to dress the part of star! I want you to have fun dressing up in clothes and accessories which express your inner star. Which brings me to another style philosophy...

[
Jaye-ism
Life is not a dress rehearsal,
so you should not be wearing
dress rehearsal clothes!
]

I love feeling like I'm being the best me I can be – **on all levels: mind, body, spirit** – and yes, FASHION! I feel it's a sign of self-respect to dress yourself so you feel like a superstar! It's energizing to swathe oneself in a velvety cashmere sweater! It's a playful high when you layer a bunch of eclectic necklaces upon your neck – each a different length, material, and design. Actually, I'm known for wearing necklaces this way, and constantly complimented for it. When I began creating my accessories line for Target, I created a super-fun layered necklace with five separate necklaces in one. You can wear each separately or in any combo. It's your choice – all dependent on your...(have you guessed the word I'm about to use?) **INTUITION**!

I also have the same passion for excess accessorizing when it comes to bracelets. The more the better. I am a big fan of layering bangles in unexpected ways. Mixing gold and silver bangles with fun cord wrap bracelets. It's not only fun to wear bracelets this way, it's a great ice breaker. Whenever I enter a room, the overwhelming response from women is I LOVE YOUR BRACELETS!

Ooooh...almost forgot! I must mention this as a recommended style tip...

[
Jaye-ism
Wear a layer of eclectic necklaces and/or bracelets to create a dramatic conversation-starter effect.
]

Another great style tip: Take a long necklace and double-duty it as a bracelet by wrapping it around your wrist. And if the necklace/bracelet can also triple-duty as a headband – bingo – you have a triple-score!

Get imaginative and re-shop your closet. Which brings me to yet another fab style tip...

[
Jaye-ism
You can save money when you find a multi purpose fashion-find.
]

Can you tell being a celeb stylist is my passion? I absolutely love offering innovative and stand-out style tips to A-list celebrities – and am now very excited to share my behind-the-red-ropes, celebrity style tips with you in this book.

Coming up ahead I will be separating the book into three main chapters:

PEOPLE
PLACES
THINGS

I feel each of these three categories are important for determining what to wear.

"THE ONLY real
VALUABLE THING
IS INTUITION."
— ALBERT EINSTEIN

For example...in the PEOPLE chapter, I will explain how it's important to suss out what **PEOPLE** mood you are in (Sexy Sirenista? Yoganista? Ingénue?) – the type of "role" you want to play in the screenplay of your life. In the **PLACES** chapter I will explain how you also dress differently depending upon the location you're heading (Starcups run? Playground run? Shopping run? Actual run?). As for the **THINGS** chapter...sometimes you will dress in a particular way simply because you're inspired by a particular must-have or lust-have object (bracelet, scarf, handbag, etc.).

Ready to get going? I sure I am. I'm looking forward to sharing all my insider secrets for attaining fabulous star-quality style – from the inside out.

xo

Jaye Hersh

PLACES   THINGS

HOLLYWOOD
[PEOPLE]
INTUITION

Nearly every woman dreams of having the life of a celebrity...starting pretty early on in life. Little girls love to dress up – play the part of movie star. This love for playing movie-star dress up never stops. It's lots of fun to wear the same looks that get celebrities lots of looks – and to be transported into a fantasy world. Coming up, I will help you explore which types of movie star icons you most relate to – and what that means about who you are within – your values, attitudes, roles, and goals. **There are 6 leading movie star icons:**

1] SIRENISTA [aka: Bombshell, Femme Fatale, Hot Mama]

2] INGÉNUE [aka: Classic Beauty, Preppy, Debutante]

3] YOGANISTA [aka: Earth Girl, All Natural Beauty, Beach Babe]

4] BOHEMIAN PRINCESS [aka: Hippy Chick, World Changer]

5] ROCK-N-ROLLER [aka: Hip Hop Babe, Grunge Girl, Technochick]

6] FASHIONISTA [aka: Trendsetter, Label Ho]

In the pages ahead, I will give you a **HOLLYWOOD SCREEN TEST** to take, which will pose all sorts of inner-guidance questions. This quiz will be both fun and enlightening – giving you feedback like a MYERS BRIGGS TEST. Afterwards you will know which movie-star icon is your dominant style personality, as well as your secondary and tertiary movie star styles. You know how you could have Leo as your main astrological sign, but have Virgo rising? Well you might have SIRENISTA as your main movie star style, then have YOGANISTA rising.

Next up, after you're done with your **HOLLYWOOD SCREEN TEST**, I will offer **INNER MAKEOVER TIPS** – advice on how to get more in touch with aspects of these movie star icons you might want to embrace more in your life. For example, if you are **not** feeling at all in touch with your SIRENISTA, I will offer some lively ideas to perk you up to feel a bit sexier – so when you dress the part of SIRENISTA, you will feel it from the inside, as well as look it on the outside. Which brings me to another of my style beliefs...

> **Jaye-ism**
> **When we feel good about ourselves, we make clearer decisions – both in fashion and in life.**

My goal for this section is to make sure you're not dressing because you hear something is IN. I want you to always be dressing because something matches WHAT'S INSIDE YOU. I've lived in Hollywood for a few decades now, and so I've witnessed how many of the girls here are bred to dress a specific part to get a reaction – strike a pose to promote a "pre-packaged-by-others" persona. Sadly, these girls start to lose their true identity – especially as they gain more celebrity status. This LOSS OF TRUE SELF especially happens when an actress becomes a lot of people's meal ticket. Some MEAL TICKET RECEIVERS might be a girl's agent, a girl's manager, or the voice of a girl's amassed fan group. And yes, even a girl's stylist can stop her from being her true core self – if the stylist doesn't tap into her **HOLLYWOOD INTUITION,** and try to enhance a girl's true inner core.

I want to drill in this reminder because I am both a celeb stylist, and a mother of a fabulous daughter. You can be sure I want my daughter to tap into her core self, and lead the life she wants – with an emphasis on her being "the leader" – not me. I never want to be an overly pushy mom. I want to give her roots and wings – as the saying goes. This same philosophy applies to how I approach being a celeb's stylist. When I take on a new celeb client, I'm wholly conscious of seeing who the girl is in her inner-core. I recognize every actress starts out with the best intentions and the sweetest of dreams. Meanwhile, the MEAL TICKET RECEIVERS have a money-making agenda which can throw a girl off course. As a celeb stylist, I always make sure [**celebrity fashion**] never becomes a drug which dizzies a girl and blurs her judgment. Fashion should always be a way to self express who you are – instead of a costume for who you think others want you to be! My insider opinion: Far too many celebrities confuse their MARKETED PERSONA for their TRUE PERSONALITY and lose themselves along the way. Even if you're not a celebrity, chances are you have a "marketed persona." Thereby you too must value prioritizing honest self-expression. All of this once again comes down to valuing your **INTUITION.** When you second-guess who you should be, you wind up with second choices in life.

I want the pages ahead to stop you from second-guessing yourself, so you can amass more of life's first choices. **So, read on...**

" KNOW YOURSELF. DON'T ACCEPT YOUR DOG'S ADMIRATION AS CONCLUSIVE EVIDENCE THAT YOU ARE WONDERFUL. "

—ANN LANDERS

are you a

[SIRENISTA?]

Bombshell, Femme Fatale, Hot Tamale, Firecracker, Vixen, Sex Kitten, Cougar, Hot Mama, or even Hot Glam-Mama?

When you walk into a room, do you sometimes think you hear the sound of clunk, clunk, clunk as collective jaws hit the floor? Wherever you are spotted – a coffee shop, a meeting, an airport – do you look as if you're either about to meet someone for a fabulous romp in bed – or as if you just exited this said scene of sublimity?

[Note: The tell-tale difference between the beforeness or afterness of these said "bedroom activities" is simply a matter of the messiness of your hairstyle. Duh.]

As a Sirenista, you're known for your clothes being vixen-like – however, your true Sirenista effect is more a matter of how comfortable you feel in your body – rather than the exact shape of your body as revealed in your clothes. Yes, that heat wave you give off when you enter a room is generated by the power of your inner confidence. If some of this sounds like you, then you're a suspect for Sirenista status. Take the following quiz to find out for sure how much of a Sirenista you may be.

HOLLYWOOD SCREEN TEST

1. Do you like to flirt for sport – with no intention of sleeping with a man?
   [A] What? You should only flirt with men you're interested in – you hussy!
   [B] I'm a lady and love it when a gent pursues me, thank you.
   [C] All the time, baby!

2. When a cute guy tosses you a sexy pick-up line you:
   [A] Blush 'n run.
   [B] Laugh 'n memorize. (Wanna giggle about it later with friends.)
   [C] Zing a sexy line back 'n memorize. (Wanna use their line later.)

3. What's your top secret weapon for magnetizing loyal fans?
   [A] My generous, compromising, sweetness.
   [B] My disciplined, together, savviness.
   [C] My sexy, mischievous, feistiness.

4. How long does it take you to hit the dance floor?
   [A] I'm more of a Dance Voyeur. Love to watch.
   [B] As much time as it takes someone to convince me or margaritas to kick in.
   [C] Same time it takes me to get from the entrance to the dancing.

5. You know what excites you sexually about as well as:
   [A] How to fix a broken nuclear generator.
   [B] How to fix a computer which always freezes.
   [C] How to direct-dial on your cellphone.

6. Your idea of kinky sex is:
   [A] Getting it on during a weeknight.
   [B] Putting something sexy on and getting it on with lights on.
   [C] Let's just say...I know the ropes.

7. When undressing in front of a man, your style most resembles:
   [A] Run and duck for the covers.
   [B] Same way I undress when shopping.
   [C] A bit of a striptease - emphasis on tease.

8. What kind of vacation sounds the most fab?
   [A] A cultural tour of some distant city.
   [B] A nature trip - like hiking in the wilderness.
   [C] The beach or a nudist colony.

9. When it comes to doing Kegels...you:
   [A] What are Kegels? That Jewish food with raisins and noodles?
   [B] The only time I do Kegels is when stuck in traffic and must pee.
   [C] I do Kegels when I remember - which reminds me, I'll do some now.

10. When someone tells you that you look especially fab, your typical response is:
    [A] "Do you want to borrow some money – whassup?"
    [B] "Thanks, but I must've looked bad last you saw me, because I don't look fab today."
    [C] "Thank you."

11. When you're smooching, your eyes are usually:
    [A] Closed. Cause I feel a bit shy.
    [B] Closed. Cause I can concentrate on those tingling sensations.
    [C] Open. I like a front-row, center view on what's unfolding.

12. You find out you have 1 month left to live... but in 100% perfect health for this month. You?
    [A] Cry a lot, prepare a will, plan a cool funeral.
    [B] Do fun G-rated things like traveling, reading books, watching TV, facebooking.
    [C] Have as much sex as humanly possible.

Once you're done with the quiz, add up how many **[C]'s** you have. What you **[C]** is what you get. If you have seven or more **[C]'s** then it's officially confirmed: you get a lot of Sirenista attention. If so, then you will want to pay particular attention to my Sirenista Style Tips up ahead.

> **WARNING:** If you don't have sexual confidence, dressing sexy can look awkward, and backfire. You really do need to feel like a Sirenista from the inside out, before you dress the part. If when answering this quiz you became reminded of your insecurities, and are eager to grow, then definitely check out the following Sirenista Boosting Tips.

Reminder #1: I believe increasing your sexual appeal can help you not only in your love life, but in your personal and professional realms. When you feel truly comfortable in your body, suddenly you will find that all the people around you feel more comfortable in your presence too.

Reminder #2: The goal of a Sirenista is not to make people nervous in your babelicious presence. Far from it. A Sirenista makes people feel more thriving and happy – hence they want to spend lots of time around fabulous you!

5 SIRENISTA BOOSTING TIPS:

[1] The time has come to make friends with that mirror mirror on your wall...intimate friends. Get naked and go stand before it. After checking out your nudey self from head to toe, look at your facial expression. Are you smiling? You should be! What do you love about your body? Smile about these parts. How is your posture? Standing taller and more perky in frame can decrease years and pounds. Decide now if there's a singular body part you want to "work on." Pick only one. Then make a plan to improve upon it. Remember: Sex appeal has far more to do with self-acceptance than your actual physical self. There will always be unchangeable aspects. Learn to love 'em cause you can't ever leave 'em.

[2] Close your eyes. Think back to when you were 8 years old. Were you accepted as your full playful, mischievous, teasing kid self? Much of being a Sirenista is feeling confidence about being: [PLAYFUL, MISCHIEVOUS, TEASING.] Make peace within yourself with any over-censoring adults from your past who tried to quell your true lively nature. Write this quote on paper and put it in a place you can see it often:

> "THE GREATEST HAZARD OF ALL, LOSING ONE'S SELF, CAN OCCUR VERY QUIETLY IN THE WORLD, AS IF IT WERE NOTHING AT ALL. NO OTHER LOSS CAN OCCUR SO QUIETLY; ANY OTHER LOSS – AN ARM, A LEG, FIVE DOLLARS, A WIFE, ETC. – IS SURE TO BE NOTICED."
> —THE SICKNESS UNTO DEATH

[3] Are you flirting with danger when it comes to men? Decide today to only allow men into your life who make you feel fabulous – not

insecure, paranoid, stressed out, and fat. Remember, as my writer friend Karen says: "You can't be your prettiest self if you have footprints on your face."

[4] Decide to take more of a dominant role in sex. Initiate it more. Make sure laughter is part of your foreplay. Try something a wee bit risque in bed – or in a whole new location nowhere near your bed.

[5] Download tunes which make you wanna get down and dirty. Music has the power not only to calm the savage breast – but also bring out your inner sexual animal. It's true. Music taps into the same pleasure centers in the brain as orgasms. Music gets your limbic system neurons all fired up, which then release calming endorphins to your brain by way of the limbic system. Translation: Sexy music literally makes you feel sexy.

COMING OUT OF THE CLOSET AS A SIRENISTA:
7 tips on dressing the hottie part

[1] Hey Sexy. Yes, you! You better start getting used to hearing "Hey Sexy" if you're gonna be and dress the part. Right now, I want you to examine your clothes and accessories. Notice which items make you feel desirable. Next time you wanna turn up the heat on your hottie self, these are your fire-em-up go-to tools.

[2] Look at which items represent depressing,

unsuccessful times. Say buh-bye to 'em! Give these items to the Salvation Army. They are hexed with disempowering energy. Let these items go! While you're at it, let go of the memories of those bad times associated with them!

[3] When you're heading out to shop for new sexy styles, keep in (your somewhat-dirty) mind, that just because clothing fits tightly, it doesn't mean it's sexy. Especially if the item makes you feel self-conscious or uncomfortable.

[4] Try to choose clothes and accessories which highlight the positive, and distract from the negative. When you know your power body part, and draw attention to this part, you create a superior sense of the sum of your parts. For example, if your boobs are your bounty, accessorize with fun necklaces. If it's your booty you want to celebrate, accessorize with cool belts.

[5] Never wear anything overtly outrageously sexy – or the item will swing around and paradoxically not be sexy at all.

[6] Confident colors can connote a sense of you as a confident canoodler. Red, black, and turquoise are a Sirenista's go-to basics.

[7] If you want more men-people to wanna touch you, pick touchable fabrics like silk, velvet, mohair, cashmere, chenille, and chiffon. If your goal is to be spanked – try leather and latex.

are you an
[INGÉNUE?]

You are sweet and innocent on the outside BUT on the inside you are...actually, you are also sweet and innocent within your adorable heart. You are a natural, classic beauty.

Sometimes your loveliness shows up in a peppy and preppy package. Sometimes as a darling and dainty debutante. You have your act together. Indeed you're nearly perfect. You're only flaw: your lack of flaws. Also, perhaps at times your tendency to be so nice to everyone might actually lead people to diagnose you as suffering from the famed [Need to Please Disease].

THE CURE: Stop caring so much what people think and want from you - and get more in touch with what YOU think and want from you.

As far as fashion goes, you pay rapt attention to what you are wearing — as do others. You're a fashion role model to many around you. You tend to dress in a way which plays it safe — so at times you can err on the side of the very predictable. Reminder: **You should be careful to wear your look — without wearing it out!**

HOLLYWOOD SCREEN TEST

1. What's in your diary?
   [A] Bawdy jokes I've overheard.
   [B] Angry thoughts on politics or people.
   [C] Gushing descriptions of who I'm crushing on.

2. When you have an appointment, you tend to arrive...
   [A] Always 15 minutes late – sorry!
   [B] It depends on traffic.
   [C] Always 15 minutes early – knowing I can relax with a good book or magazine to read.

3. Do you have lots of friends?
   [A] Just a few close friends.
   [B] Lots of friends – and we love going out as a loud group.
   [B] I'm friendly with a big group, but only close with a few.

4. Which of these best describes your bedroom?
   [A] Messy. Stop! Don't go in there!
   [B] Sexy and ready for action.
   [C] Neat and orderly – with lots of feminine touches.

5. Your fingernails can best be described as:
   [A] Bitten Paws.
   [B] Kitten Claws.
   [C] Neat and Clean.

6. When you have your mani/pedi you choose...
   [A] Gothalicious black.
   [B] Cherry red.
   [C] Champagne pink.

7. How far ahead have you planned your life?
   [A] I've figured out the next few months.
   [B] I live in the moment, baby.
   [C] I have a strategic five-year plan, thanks!

8. When you've had a long day, how do you relax?
   [A] Read my favorite book or watch TV.
   [B] Round up a big group of friends and party hearty!
   [C] Chill out at home with a homemade meal, a movie, and a loved one.

9. You consider your birthday...
   [A] The day I was born.
   [B] A day to get drunk on dirty martinis till I pass out in my birthday cake.
   [C] An important emotional milestone for reflection.

10. What types of movies do you prefer?
    [A] Raucous comedies.
    [B] Action-packed adventures.
    [C] Happy, romantic story lines.

11. When you're sad, your favorite cuddle-bunny is:
    [A] A good hardcover book.
    [B] A good stiff drink.
    [C] My sweetie (but I'm not the type to make a joke about him being hard or stiff).

12. What pet would you most likely own?
    [A] Ferret or snake.
    [B] Golden retriever.
    [C] Persian cat.

Once you're done with the quiz, add up how many **[C]'s** you have. What you **[C]** is what you get. If you have seven or more **[C]'s** then it's officially confirmed: you are a sweet thang Ingénue. If so, then you will want to pay particular attention to my Ingénue Style Tips up ahead.

> **WARNING:** Excessive "people-pleasing" can be extremely damaging to your emotional well-being. As an Ingénue you tend to never want to break rules. With this in mind, I recognize you will have the instant urge to follow all my recommended fashion rules perfectly to a tee. But one of my rules I now want to give you is to break some of my fashion rules – while being careful not to break any nails, of course! It's good to break your pattern of being a good girl every now and then. A little rebellion will be good for your spirit.

Reminder: One of the most fabulous aspects of being an Ingénue is your big heart. I want you know that the world needs more kind and empathic people like you – and we appreciate your presence on this planet. Your bright smile is contagious – so keep on flashing it.

5 INGÉNUE BOOSTING TIPS:

[1] If you wanna renew your Ingénue sensibilities, go forth and do more good deeds. You can use your big, warm heart to do something about global warming. Did you know that during the 20th century, the average surface temperature of the world has increased by up to 1.4°F? Yikes. You can help by...

A] Using compact fluorescent bulbs. Look around your home. Which lights in your home do you use the most? Replace them with compact fluorescent bulbs. Three CFBs will save 300 lbs. of carbon dioxide and $60 per year!

B] Inflating Your Tires! If you maintain your tires, you can save $840 per year and keep 250 lbs. of carbon dioxide out of the air!

C] Fill the dishwasher. Run your dishwasher only when it's full. That'll save $40 and 100 lbs. of carbon dioxide emission a year.

[2] Look at your schedule book – and suss out where you can cut back and slow down – because a true Ingénue is trying to be a good girl to everyone. It's time to learn how to pronounce that tongue-twister of a word: Noooooooo.

[3] Shut up and meditate. As a people-pleaser, you need to silence your mind more, so you can better hear your true inner voice. Write down and post this quote someplace you can see it often:

> "Any life, no matter how long and complex it may be, is made up of a single moment – the moment in which a man finds out, once and for all, who he is."
>
> –Jorge Luis Borges

[4] You love to smile – and the world smiles along with you. I want to make sure you protect your smile muscles – plus take some time for self-care after running around helping out everyone else. So here's a fabulous homemade facial mask to use regularly – great for all skin types. It's simple to make – as **it has only two ingredients:**

   *__1 tbsp. natural yogurt,__ room temperature [not lowfat or non-fat]

   *__1 tsp. runny honey__ [microwave to soften hardened honey]

Mix it up, then apply to face. Let sit for 15 minutes. Wash your face with steaming washcloth.

[5] Download tunes which help keep you feeling happy and peppy and giddy. Show tunes. Brazilian Music. Reggae.

COMING OUT OF THE CLOSET AS AN INGÉNUE:
4 tips on dressing the sweetie pie part

[1] I know you presently have all your clothes neatly folded and hanging nice and organized. But I'd love for you to ransack your bureaus and closets and locate the clothes and accessories you tend to wear the most. Be honest with yourself. Do you own too much pink? Too many turtlenecks? The time has come to still keep your sugary sweetness – but add some spice. Chocolate-brown spice is a good new color place to start. Chocolate brown is a wonderful color which goes fabulously with pink – and is still soft and conservative in its own right. Olive green is also a good color complement to your pretty in pink wardrobe tendencies. **Make a list of what you want to buy to go with what you already own.**

[2] I know since you're an Ingénue that you have a good soul. Let's make sure you have good soles as well. Go to your closet and take a good long look at your shoes. Hold their toes up to your nose. Are they scuffed? Next take a feel of those heels. Have you been running around trying to help people out so very much that you've worn those heels into little chipped stubs? Create a pile of shoes which need a little tender loving shoe-care – then bring them to the repair guy.

[3] Do you have pretty, sleeveless, silky summer dresses you love – but feel you can only have summer lovin' for? You can love these summer darlings all year round. Simply slip a tee or a long sleeve Danskin or jersey beneath this sleeveless frock – and voila – your love for this pretty ditty will no longer be stopped by seasonal boundaries!

[4] You're always sticking your neck out to help others. You want to decorate that sleek and slender neck of yours to perfection with a pretty scarf. A fun way to wear a scarf is to wrap the scarf around your neck backwards to forwards...then keep wrapping the scarf around your neck as many times as you can.

[YOGANISTA?]

You don't want to be defined – as you are always grow-ing. You are always searching for who you are – and why you are here on this planet. You see yourself as a bit of the following:

Earth Girl, All Natural Beauty, Beach Babe, Spiritual Diva, Peace Goddess, Lover of Light, Truth, and Forgiveness!

You are curious about becoming more spiritually awake. You are eager to learn how to put aside your limiting beliefs. You are striving to live each day by looking neither too far backward nor too far forward – striving instead to be fully present in the moment. You feel you have a purpose for being here on this planet – and WANT TO CREATE A POSITIVE RIPPLE EFFECT BY YOUR PRESENCE – spreading love, hap-piness, and peace forward to all whom you encounter. You appreciate beauty – not just in nature – but every-where. Indeed, you can revel in the loveliness of a lake as much as the gorgeousness of a crystal necklace or a new pair of shoes. You are always pointing out beautiful people, things, objects, and ideas to others – which they don't ever notice. You are a noticer.

Shape. Color. Light. Texture. Smell. Sound. Patterns. You notice them all – and revel in their various beauties.

HOLLYWOOD SCREEN TEST

1. When you hear yet another news story about the chaotic state of our world, you...
   [A] Turn it off by switching to a sitcom.
   [B] Turn it down by paying attention to your magazine.
   [C] Turn it into conversation.

2. You're at a park and see a little girl crying – while her parents don't notice. You...
   [A] Me? Not my responsibility!
   [B] Approach the parents and yell at the creeps.
   [C] Approach the parents and kindly point out the situation.

3. If a friend cancelled plans on you at the last moment, you would...
   [A] Feel sad and mad worrying what it meant.
   [B] Recognize I have a GET OUT OF PLAN FREE CARD to cancel on 'em!
   [C] Not worry. Things happen. Forgive. Forget.

4. If you knew two close friends were fighting, you would...
   [A] Act as Judge Judy – figure out who's right and who wins!
   [B] Let them settle their dispute eventually.
   [C] Warmly help each see the other's POV.

5. Your favorite drink of choice is:
   [A] A Dirty Martini/ Cosmo/Sex on The Beach.
   [B] Frappuccino/Red Bull/Double Espresso.
   [C] Chai Tea/Fruit Smoothie/Coconut Water.

6. Love is:
   [A] ...A pain in the heart! Fun – until somebody gets hurt!
   [B] ...Fab if you mean "making" it, mixed if your feeling it.
   [C] ...Why we are here! To get better at learning to love!

7. You sometimes feel so connected to people, it feels as if there is no separation between you/them.
   [A] What the heck are you talking about?
   [B] When in love, I feel that way about my mate.
   [C] Yes – and I love the feeling of that sense of oneness.

8. You're lost in a hood you've never been to. You...
   [A] Snap to attention. Take control. Give directions.
   [B] Worry if you'll ever get to where you're going.
   [C] Stay relaxed. It's an adventure! Stop friendly pedestrians to ask directions.

9. If you could live anywhere, you'd live in...
   [A] Any affluent neighborhood close to great dining and shopping.
   [B] Any nice suburb close to good schools.
   [C] Any place close to gorgeous nature settings.

10. Do you make others carry your luggage?
    [A] Duh. I am a girl.
    [B] How insulting. Just because I'm a girl, I can still carry luggage!
    [C] I can carry my bags. I'm strong and travel lightly. But I'm open to help.

11. Your thoughts on going camping are:
    [A] For me camping is staying at a hotel which is under four stars.
    [B] As long as there's a nearby hotel to shower and blow dry my hair.
    [C] Love watching the night sky with my sweetie.

12. Do you check your makeup more than 2X daily?
    [A] At least twice every few hours.
    [B] I try to. Why, is my makeup smudged now?
    [C] I don't wear much makeup – so there's not much to check.

Once you're done with the quiz, add up how many [C]'s you scored. What you [C] is what you get. If you have seven or more [C]'s then it officially confirmed: you are a Yoganista. If so, then you will want to pay particular attention to my Yoganista Style Tips coming up.

> **WARNING:** Just because you are a down-to-earth gal, there's no excuse to let yourself get too care-free about your hair, cleanliness, and "clothing-rumpleness-quotient." Taking the time to care about style and fashion is not a superficial thing. How beautifully you represent yourself to the world shows how much self-love you have – and is yet another form of self-expression. "Self-love" and "self-expression" are two strong character values you seek to uphold. Like everything in life, it's a matter of moderation. You don't have to make fashion your number-one reason for living. But you can make living your gorgeous life feel more gorgeous if you are feeling at your utmost gorgeous on a daily basis. Be sure you are not giving yourself too many excuses about not getting "dressed up" to go out. **Your goal: Represent your "inner beauty" as fully as you can – by being at your utmost beautiful on the outside.**

4 YOGANISTA BOOSTING TIPS:

Here is an inspiring story from my writer friend, Karen Salmansohn, that is a great Yoganista booster: *A rabbi and his disciple were walking in the street when a fancy carriage dangerously careened towards them. The angry man inside began shouting insulting words at the rabbi and his disciple to get out of his way.*

The rabbi landed in a ditch, then yelled "May you have everything you want!" The disciple asked, "Rabbi, why did you say that to a man with such horrible behavior?" The rabbi replied, "Because a happy man wouldn't throw a rabbi into a ditch."

As a Yoganista, you want to be sure you are beautiful both inside and out. This means you must maintain a sense of inner peace and love for others. Granted, life is always challenging us to remain peaceful and loving. You must recognize, however, that anger and resentment are toxic. They give you frown lines – which even the most ardent Botox seeker will have a hard time combating! With this in mind, below are **INNER MAKEOVER TIPS** to help you maintain your inner Yoganista beauty.

[1] Start each day with a "Love Meditation." Close your eyes. Become aware of your breath. Tell yourself with every breath, you're breathing out anger, breathing in love.

[2] Whenever you're feeling toxic anger tell yourself: "We are all good, loving souls who occasionally get lost." Think about the rabbi in the story. Pray for your offending person to find their way.

[3] When you're feeling anxious, tell yourself: "I cannot always control what goes on outside. But I can control what goes on inside." Hone in on one of these mantras to repeat throughout your day: **love is why we're here; everything's for a reason; onward and upward.**

[4] Still having trouble forgiving? Remind yourself of a time you were forgiven. Be altruistic. Forgive back to your offending person. Know: When you resent someone you are giving them control of your emotions!

COMING OUT OF THE CLOSET AS A YOGANISTA:
3 tips for dressing the spiritual diva part

[1] Be honest about what you love and wear. Toss what doesn't "speak to you." As a Yoganista you will appreciate the perks of this "Letting Go Exercise." Tossing old clothes trains your brain to get rid of old thoughts and ideas. Psychologists say that you can train your brain to feel more comfortable about "change" – by starting with easy changes – like throwing out old clothes. Basically, when you make simple changes you associate "change" with "hmmmm, that was easy." When you throw out clothes in a closet, you're also visually seeing how you're making extra space for new, exciting things to come into your life – another positive association for change!

[2] You're all about stretching yourself outside of comfort zones. And so I want you to buy one new thing – which is very much about who you are – but still pushes you to grow. Maybe this piece of clothing is a bit sexier than you're used to wearing. Push thyself. Grow thyself.

[3] You're in favor of transformation. You can easily transform even the most simple outfit into a knockout by adding dangling necklaces and bracelets. Experiment with adding stunning colorful gems. Turquoise and pink gemstones look fabulous together. Also... consider the following power and meanings of the gemstones you choose:

Citrine: Helps to manifest your goals and attracts abundance.

Coral: A good stimulant for the root chakra. Protects you from depression.

Emerald: Helps communication; good for discovering the truth in the chaos of information.

Jade: Helps you accept things which are difficult.

Lapis: Helps you quiet your mind and brings on insights and creativity.

Malachite: Helps you with the heart chakra – known for bringing on psychic visions.

Rose Quartz: Opens up the heart for both giving and receiving love.

Ruby: Strengthens love, self-esteem, loyalty, and bravery.

Tiger Eye: Helps you to become more flexible in your beliefs.

Turquoise: Famed for being able to draw out negative vibrations.

are you a
[BOHEMIAN]
PRINCESS?]

You embrace style in your own eclectic, one-of-a-kind way. Just as you prefer indie movies to mass-market ones, you prefer indie designers to mass-market ones. You speak your independent mind – but with femininity and warmth.

You don't like to make waves. But you do delight in inviting people to lull around in the wavy waters – because, hey, it's so much more fun and playful where the waves are! You're not one to dip a toe into those waves either. You jump right on in.

You're always thinking outside the box – and this applies to political boxes, music boxes, art boxes – and yes fashion boxes.

When a clothing store is having a sale on the things they couldn't sell, you will often lovelovelove these items — because they were a little offbeat. You like mixing modern indie-designer clothes with quirky vintage finds. You're a Hippy Dippy Chick in many ways – but no Granola Girl. You prefer yummy five-grain, steel-cut, oatmeal with caramelized bananas and real-deal, 100% maple syrup. Your nutritionist suggests you have a bowl with your coffee (with soy), because it will lessen your glycemic dip. YOU'RE DOWN TO EARTH, BUT KNOW SUCH PRINCESS THINGS.

HOLLYWOOD SCREEN TEST

1. You want to see an indie movie...but no friends want to go. Your thoughts?
   [A] I figure the movie must be bad, so don't go.
   [B] I bribe a friend by paying for her ticket - or go with someone I don't like.
   [C] I go it alone. Gotta see that flick, dammit!

2. When you buy ice cream you usually choose...
   [A] The same favored flavor every time.
   [B] The flavor with the least calories.
   [C] The newest flavor.

3. Do you typically wear a watch?
   [A] Yes. I need to be on schedule.
   [B] No. I have my cellphone for the time.
   [C] Yes. If it's a super cool watch. But I love it for its stylin' not its schedulin'.

4. When someone takes a long time to express their thoughts, you...
   [A] Get friggin frustrated.
   [B] Patiently, silently listen.
   [C] Encourage them to open up with jokes and loving words.

5. Which is the most true for you about mistakes?
   [A] It's hard to admit - or think about - being wrong.
   [B] If logic prevails, I will begrudgingly admit my mistakes.
   [C] I'm open to admitting mistakes because I'm open to growing!

6. When it comes to mainstream music, TV, movies...
   [A] I love that stuff!
   [B] I am highly discerning and will never watch mass garbage.
   [C] I much prefer indie - but admit there's good mainstream. I like to mix it up.

7. You openly express opinions that are controversial or plain old weird.
   [A] Never.
   [B] Sometimes, but it makes me feel awkward.
   [C] Often - and it leads to fantastic conversations and deeper connections.

8. You love to break the rules and do things your way, even if this means less friends...
   [A] Always. People suck a lot of the time anyway - especially if they don't accept me as I am.
   [B] Never. What's the point of losing friends?
   [C] I value my POV and friendships equally - so try to live honestly while keeping the peace.

9. When talking to people your body language is:
   [A] Standing with my arms folded.
   [B] Talking with my hands a little - or having one or both hands on my hips.
   [C] Touching the other person - waving my hands - playing with my hair. I'm expressive.

10. Do you have any unique hobbies or obscure interests?
    [A] Nope.
    [B] One.
    [C] More than one. I love discovering the unusual.

11. When something really amuses you, your reaction is...
    [A] A silent laugh, and small smile.
    [B] Saying aloud: "Now that's funny."
    [C] An appreciative hearty laugh.

12. You tend to spend long periods of time alone...
    [A] Rarely. I need and love being around people.
    [B] Sometimes - but quickly miss people.
    [C] Often. If I'm doing something I passionately love, I lose track of time and missing people.

Finito with that Bohemian Princess quiz? Time to add up how many [C]'s you have. Again, what you [C] is what you got goin' on. If you have seven or more [C]'s then it's officially confirmed: you are christened a Bohemian Princess. If so, then you will want to pay particular attention to my Bohemian Princess tips below.

Reminder: I recognize that you don't like to look like everyone else – so you're going to be fearful of following my prescribed style tips. Please know I want you to follow your intuition and embrace only what feels right for your iconoclastic and classy Bohemian Princess sensibilities. Chances are you probably even have some amazing self-invented style tips I could benefit from knowing about. If you feel you do, I'd be up for hearing your ideas. Please write to me at my store – or drop on by. The address is: 10581 WEST PICO BOULEVARD, LOS ANGELES, CA 90064...

BOHEMIAN PRINCESS BOOSTING STORY:

Karen Salmansohn, my writer, told me this story – and it's a fabulous story to boost the inner spirit of Bohemian Princesses.

Once upon a time there was this girl (Lisa) who was walking along the beach...when she saw what appeared to be a genie bottle in the sand. She bent down, and on a what-the-heck whim, rubbed the bottle. Sure enough a genie came floating out. **"Geez, it's claustrophobic in there,"** *the genie said.* **"Thanks for getting me out. In appreciation, I will grant you one wish." "Hey! Isn't it three wishes?"** *Lisa asked.* **"No, no, it's just one,"** *said the genie.* **"Hmm,"** *said Lisa.* **"How about if I make my one wish that I get three wishes?" "Sorry, honey,"** *said the genie,* **"I'm onto that trick. It's just one wish. And while you're deciding, can I borrow your sunblock. It's so bright and hot out here."** *Begrudgingly Lisa handed the genie her sunblock, while she pondered what one wish she wanted most. She could ask for a mansion in Malibu. That would be fun. Or a sexy guy. Or she could ask to look ten years younger, ten pounds thinner. No wait, she reminded herself, she could only pick one wish. Damn this genie. And that's when it hit her. SHE FOUND A GENIE LOOPHOLE!* **"You ready yet, honey?"** *the genie prodded.* **"Yes, I'm ready,"** *said Lisa,* **"I now know what to ask for to get every wish I could think of. My wish is to be happy. Because happiness is REALLY what I'm looking for in every wish I can think up. So, when you grant me happiness I'll actually be getting everything I want in one wish." "Not bad,"** *said the genie.* **"You're a smart gal!" "Thanks."** *said Lisa,* **"Oh, and I love your genie outfit! Did you get that at JAYE HERSH'S store INTUITION?"** *Then the genie laughed.* **"Trade secret where I got this outfit. And here's another secret! There's another wish you could have asked** *for before your brilliant wish. You could ask to truly know yourself through and through. Because the more you know yourself, the better you know what to seek to make you most happy."* The one big Bohemian Princess boosting tip: Know thyself and always seek one-of-a-kind personal happiness.

COMING OUT OF THE CLOSET AS A BOHEMIAN PRINCESS:
3 tips on dressing like down-to-earth royalty

[1] Take a gander at your wardrobe and brainstorm how to goose it up! What pieces of clothes and accessories have you yet to introduce to one another? Play matchmaker, matchmaker, make yourself a new match. Fix up a new combo you've yet to try! Introduce something vintage to something modern – and something lacy to something leathery. Team up a range of assorted necklaces and wear them all at the same time with a simple tee and jeans.
[2] If you're low on cash and high on creativity, spend extra time in vintage shops and Salvation Army stores to buy inexpensive items to mix and match with your expensive indie-designer tastes. When shopping, always choose clothes and accessories in the same way you might choose a romantic partner. Never pick to please your friends. Instead be highly aware of choosing items which truly

complement THE REAL YOU – items which make you feel most confident and happy.
[3] DON'T BE A REBEL WITHOUT A CLUE! I know you like to push the envelope with your one-of-a-kind fashion look – but there are some universal major celebrity no-no-NO's – HOLLYWOULDn'TS – you should adhere to.

HOLLYWOULDn'TS
a] HOLEY LEGGINGS on anyone over 30-ISH.

B] HOLEY JEANS on anyone over 45.

C] FULL SKIRTS WITH COWBOY BOOTS – unless you are square dancing.

D] DIRTY BRA STRAPS – ever – and especially not showing under a tank top.

e] PANTS TOO LOW – PANTIES TOO HIGH...

F] STRUTTING IN HIGH HEELS YOU CLEARLY CANNOT WALK IN.

G] SPORTING a HANDBAG WITH BROKEN HARDWARE.

H] BUTTON-UP BLOUSE POPPING AT THE BRA LINE.

I] DEODORANT STAINS ON a BLACK TEE SHIRT.

are you a

[ROCK-N-ROLLER?]

Are your hills alive with the sound of the following music: **Nirvana, Sonic Youth, Amy Winehouse, L7, Bikini Kill, Jack White, Babes in Toyland, Kanye, The Strokes, Yeah Yeah Yeahs, Beastie Boys, The Flaming Lips, and Green Day?**

Do you make your own rules – then break your own rules? Do you have a difficult time passing through airport metal detectors because of all the metal embellishments you are wearing? Are your jeans one of your main "fashion staples" – and should these jeans of yours be literally stapled, because they're ripped and falling apart? Do you love that famed expression "What other people think of me is none of my business?" Are you right now thinking: [ENOUGH QUESTIONS DAMMIT!] If you're nodding your head – and your nodding head is sporting hair which is messy – then chances are you're a Rock-N-Roller chick. You dress as if you have just left the stage from a performance. Indeed, the world is your stage for fun and laughter. You don't particularly look at labels or pay attention to current trends. These are for "posers," which you are anything but.

You have your own unique style – although you do love looking at pics of Courtney Love, Kat Bjelland, Kathleen Hanna, Donita Sparks, Amy Winehouse, and Mia Zapata.

HOLLYWOOD SCREEN TEST

1. I say Nirvana. You say:
   [A] Chocolate.
   [B] Kurt Cobain was sexy. How the heck did Courtney land him?
   [C] One of the best grunge bands ever!

2. Do you wish Fred Durst would die in a pool of his own vomit?
   [A] Who's Fred Durst?
   [B] That's gross, now I am about to vomit.
   [C] Yes! High Five.

3. If you were in a band, you would sing about...
   [A] How love is beautiful.
   [B] How I shot the sheriff – but I have a good alibi about the deputy.
   [C] Heartache, pain, loneliness – you know, stuff detailing what my day was like.

4. Are you more passive or aggressive?
   [A] Passive. I'm all about Peace, Love, and Understanding.
   [B] It's a swing vote depending upon my time of the month.
   [C] Aggressive – what of it? Is that a problem?

5. What do you think of grunge music?
   [A] Um...er...what is it?
   [B] Not my thing.
   [C] It's the soundtrack to my life.

6. How often do you do your laundry?
   [A] My maid does it.
   [B] Once a week.
   [C] Once every month or two months.

7. What do you think of ripped jeans?
   [A] Tacky and you could ruin a manicure in them.
   [B] Fun occasionally.
   [C] LOVE them – but if you buy expensive, pre-ripped, you're a poser.

8. Your thoughts on eyeliner are:
   [A] Nice every now and then.
   [B] Too much is a bad thing.
   [C] Love it: thick, dark, dramatic!

9. You love to break the rules and do things your way, even if this means less friends.
   [A] Never. What's the point of losing friends?
   [B] I value my POV and friendships equally – so try to live honestly while keeping peace.
   [C] Always. People suck a lot of the times anyway – especially if they don't accept me as I am.

10. The color black is:
    [A] Appropriate for funerals.
    [B] Slenderizing and classy for cocktail parties.
    [C] Black is the new black – and eternally cool for EVERY outing!

11. You get into fights when...
    [A] I'm visiting home for family holidays – then feel guilty.
    [B] I'm PMSing or stressed – then feel bad.
    [C] Someone says something dumb – which is a lot – then feel energized.

12. Do you ever get pissed off when someone mixes you up with a Goth?
    [A] Excuse me? That's never happened.
    [B] Once again – excuse me?
    [C] Yes! I hate when that happens!

Finito with that quiz-o? Now add up how many **[C]**'s you have. What you **[C]** is who you be! If you have seven or more **[C]**'s you're officially confirmed as a Rock-N-Roller babe. If so, then you will want to pay particular attention to my Rock-N-Roller Style Tips up ahead.

[44

WARNING: I know you're not fond of authority and police of any kind – including The Fashion Police. But, with that said, I'd love to encourage you to read on so as to make sure if your band hits the big time you don't wind up in the "**WHAT WAS SHE THINKING WHEN SHE WORE THAT?**" section of **PEOPLE** or **INSTYLE MAGAZINE.**

5 ROCK-N-ROLLER BOOSTING TIPS:

If you want to feel more like a Rock-N-Roller girl, you gotta get your feelings more stirred up, from the inside out! So...

1. Put on your favorite playlist and turn up the volume.

2. Read this womanifesto which sums up the strong feelings of a Rock-N-Roller girl.

3. Write down your top womanifestos. Post them. Read them. Feel them often!

4. Consider writing a song about one or two of them.

5. Express yourself to a tee! Buy some simple white tees and colorful permanent markers. Write your favorite statements on the tees. If you want to draw a pic too, go crazy!

rock-n-roller womanifesto:

- I FEEL STRONGLY ABOUT NOT WANTING TO FIT INTO ANY MOLD!
- I FEEL STRONGLY THAT BIGOTS SHOULD SPONTANEOUSLY COMBUST!
- I FEEL STRONGLY THAT SEXISM, RACISM, AND HOMOPHOBIA ARE RETRO! LET'S STOP IT ALREADY, DAMMIT!
- I FEEL STRONGLY THAT I SHOULD BE ABLE TO BE MY SEXIEST SELF AND NOT FEAR OBJECTIFICATION OR ASSAULT!
- I FEEL STRONGLY THAT WOMEN IN OTHER COUNTRIES SHOULD HAVE MORE RIGHTS AND WE NEED TO HELP THEM!
- I FEEL STRONGLY ABOUT MY LOVE FOR ZINES, WEBSITES, AND BLOGS!
- I FEEL STRONGLY ABOUT WANTING MORE PEOPLE TO BE MORE GLOBALLY AWARE!
- I FEEL STRONGLY THAT AWARENESS ITSELF IS NOT ENOUGH – THERE'S TOO MUCH TALK AND NOT ENOUGH ACTION!
- I FEEL STRONGLY ABOUT NEEDING MORE PEOPLE TO HELP OUR EARTH!
- I FEEL STRONGLY THAT GIRLS AREN'T HERE SIMPLY TO LOOK PRETTY!
- I FEEL STRONGLY THAT GIRLS CAN CHANGE THIS PLANET!
- I FEEL STRONGLY ABOUT WANTING TO DO MY PART TO CHANGE THIS PLANET!
- I FEEL STRONGLY ABOUT D.I.Y. (DOING IT YOURSELF)!

COMING OUT OF THE CLOSET AS A ROCK-N-ROLLER:
6 tips on how to dress the grunge grrrrl part

[1] If you love ripped jeans, but don't love feeling like a cold grrrrl in those brrrrr winter months, wear pajama pants under them.

[2] During the summer, buy three quarter jeans, which are not too baggy, then rip up the ends where the fold is, using a sharp object. Or simply burn the ends with a lighter – within your kitchen sink – so if things get too fiery you can splash water ASAP.

[3] Rock-N-Roller girls love to have their style look made with the shades. Black sunglasses are theeeee best. But nevah–evah sports shades! The old Blues Brothers ones are fab – as are the big round sunglasses like the ones Kurt and/or Jackie O were known for sporting.

[4] Hats are fun to wear – that is if they don't look squeaky clean. If they do, throw them in the wash a few times. Or if it's a baseball hat, mess it up a bit. If it's a toque, cut it up a bit.

[5] Rock-N-Roller girls love to make big statements with their eyes/lips. Be forewarned: pick 1 of the 2 at a time. If you're expressing with your eyes, make your eyeliner prominent and thick – but also casually smudged – as if you've slept in it. If it's your lips you're highlighting, always test the lipstick on your lips not your hand before you buy – especially if you're seeking a risky dark color.

[6] TRY DYE YOUR HAIR WITH KOOL-AID

a] Determine if bleaching is necessary. Blondes don't need to bleach, but brunettes and redheads will – for a noticeable color change. And, if you do have red hair, Kool-Aid dyeing may not work. And if you have dark hair, but all you're looking for is a color tint, you can skip the bleaching.

b] Bleaching is simple, if you buy a bleach kit from the store. You want a kit that specifically states bleaching. A blonding kit is not enough. Follow the instructions – **except DO NOT use the conditioner that comes with the kit.** This will close off your hair to the Kool-Aid color.

c] Choose a fun and bright Kool-Aid color you love. Mix 2 packets of unsweetened mix with a double quarter sized amount of conditioner.

Note: it's important you use unsweetened Kool-Aid. If you use the sugar–added type, your hair will be a total mess.

d] If you haven't just bleached your hair, wet it. Put on plastic gloves. Apply Kool-Aid mixture. Place plastic wrap on head. Leave it all on as long as you can – even all day.

Note: the longer you leave it all on, the stronger your color result!

e] Over time, the Kool-Aid color naturally fades out. If you want it out speedier, try a little toothpaste to speed up the process.

are you a [FASHIONISTA?]

You're often late to meet people because you can't decide between Mary Janes and moccasins. You either have started (or have considered starting) to keep a diary of what you wore to what event so you don't dare ever repeat an outfit. You live, breathe, and obsess over the latest style must-haves and lust-haves. You are on more than one wait list for a hard-to-get fashion item. You have even been known to bribe and/or do special favors to get yourself on a faster inside track to snagging that latest [IT-BAG] or "one-of-a-kind leather bomber." You are the first in line for the latest weekly celebrity and fashion magazines so you can have the 411 on the latest and greatest. You pride yourself on having the insider scoop and the coolest goods before anyone else even whiffs them in the air.

You are a Trendsetter, A Label Ho, A Fashion Mentor – and voted most likely to inspire a <u>Single White Female</u> imitator to follow your fashion lead fabulousness.

HOLLYWOOD SCREEN TEST

1. How would you describe your fashion sense?
   [A] **Casual and comfy.**
   [B] **Pretty Good.**
   [C] **Impeccable.**

2. Your dream vacation would be:
   [A] **Camping in Yosemite.**
   [B] **Skiing in Aspen.**
   [C] **New York for fashion week or Paris for big fashion shows.**

3. What would you do with a Pashmina Wrap?
   [A] **Add ketchup.**
   [B] **Wear it. Love it!**
   [C] **Been there, wrapped that! Buh-bye!**

4. Boots are made for:
   [A] **Hiking.**
   [B] **Snowy or rainy weather.**
   [C] **Cat walkin'.**

5. How would you like your partner to dress?
   [A] **What he wears often makes me wince – but hey at least I know he's hetero.**
   [B] **Sweats and a hoodie are his norm.**
   [C] **He's got great style – which makes me smile!**

6. What jewelry would you wear to a pool party?
   [A] **I wouldn't wear jewelry.**
   [B] **Maybe a necklace – which I would take off if swimming.**
   [C] **A toe ring and anklet – looks sexy when dipping feet in the water.**

7. You are meeting your girlfriends at the mall for lunch. You wear...
   [A] **Whatever my friends are wearing.**
   [B] **Something casual and comfy.**
   [C] **A fabulous outfit – and do something fun with my hair.**

8. Your closet is:
   [A] **A messy disorganized chaos trap.**
   [B] **Sparse within.**
   [C] **Heaven on earth.**

9. What would you be watching out of these choices on TV?
   [A] **I don't watch TV.**
   [B] **A hit sitcom or hit drama.**
   [C] <u>**Project Runway**</u> **or Tyra Banks or some other fashion show.**

10. You often dream that you are:
    [A] **Searching for somebody.**
    [B] **Flying or floating.**
    [C] **Shopping, or in a fashion show, or wearing something fabulous.**

11. What dog would you most like to own?
    [A] **Golden retriever.**
    [B] **Mutt dog from the local shelter.**
    [C] **Chihuahua or something adorably petite.**

12. You've just been through a tough breakup. You...
    [A] **Go for a run or do massive yoga.**
    [B] **One word: chocolate.**
    [C] **Two words: retail therapy.**

Hi again. Curious to know how many [C]'s you have. What you [C] is what you dress. If you have seven or more [C]'s then it's official: you, my sweet one, are a Fashionista. If so, then you will want to check out some of my Fashionista Style Tips up ahead.

WARNING #1: Clothes are your drug. If you don't watch out they can become a very expensive drug habit – especially if you try to change your whole wardrobe each season. Fashionistas should consider following a 70/30 rule: 70% classic pieces, 30% new trendy pieces. Also – consider paying for your Style Drugs like a real druggie does – with cash only! It will give you an instant real life sense of how much moolah you're spending.

WARNING #2: Do not do your budget or body undue harm! Know what looks good on one-of-a-kind you. Just because a cool new style looks fabulous in a magazine or TV show doesn't mean it's gonna be a fashion delight for you.

3 FASHIONISTA BOOSTING TIPS:

[1] Keep up to date on the latest trends by reading all the coolest fashion magazines. For a Fashionista, these are like porn magazines. They will get you truly in the mood to shop! As for the equivalent of porn video, be sure watch TLC and WHAT NOT TO WEAR and as many fashion TV shows as possible!
[2] Start friendly conversations with sales people at your favorite boutiques. Ask them

what they're seeing and loving in new styles – and what exciting new finds are on the horizon for their store! Sales people also offer terrific inside-information sources about upcoming sales – and can often slip you an extra discount if they feel you're a Fashionista with a big heart and limited budget.
[3] Are you a Fashionista on a budget? Do you want to look like money without spending too much money? If so, here's some empowering ideas.
a] Keep a shopping list. This will help reduce unnecessary splurges and keep your budget focused on pumping up your wardrobe with the coolest most needed goodies.
b] Pepper up your wardrobe's "70% classic pieces" by buying new trendy accessories to make them appear new, and off-the-hook. You can also purchase "shoe jewelry" to inexpensively switch up the look of simple pump shoes.
c] Amortize your amour for expensive items! Figure out what the "Object of Your Obsession" will **cost you per wear**. For example, if you spend $800.00 on an incredible, warm winter coat – and you wear it most of the winter – and even a few winters thereafter – then it's just an inexpensive, pennies-a-day purchase. However if you spend $800.00 on one groovy dress you plan to wear only once or twice – and it might not be fashionable come next year – well, then, that's a pricey purchase.
d] Recycle trendy styles by heading off to

grandmother's house. Generously suggest to help grandma clean out her clothing closet. You might be surprised by how much you love what she was wearing a few generations ago! You go, grandma!

e] Set up a SWAP AND SHOP with fellow Fashionista's – where you create a clothing swap with each other's forgotten favorites. One girl's presently under-appreciated Prada is another girl's new go-to item. Also, being around other Fashionista's can bring you insider-access to what's new, what's hot, and what's on sale!

COMING OUT OF THE CLOSET AS A FASHIONISTA:
get in touch with your inner/outer trendy self

[1] Not only do styles have expiration dates – so do cosmetics! They can go "bad" by either changing color or becoming infectious. Every six months be sure to toss old foundations, mascaras, and eye liners.

[2] Love your beloved fashion finds with tender loving care. For example, properly hand wash those cashmere sweaters and for lingerie use cold water/hair conditioner! And be sure to only dry-clean those dry-clean onlies!

[3] Want to try to maintain that recommended 70%/30% rule with those "70% classic pieces" – but you don't know much about what "classic pieces" means? Voila...

YOUR 70% CLASSIC PIECES LIST:

a] The perfect little black dress – it should be made of a quality lightweight fabric like a cotton/rayon blend. Avoid heavy wools which can plump up your look and limit your seasonal wear.

b] One fabulous black suit – make it a seasonless material like gabardine or rayon.

c] One gorgeous white button-down shirt. Wear it beneath tees or with suits.

d] One stunning pair of black pumps – make the heel walkable in height – so those pumps can walk you from the office to dinner.

e] Well-fitting jeans – particularly dark denim, which tends to be more slenderizing and consistently more stylish than lighter color denims.

f] Chinos/brown pants/black pants/khakis – when you wanna switch over from jeans, to something still casual – voila!

g] A few fun tees. White, black, and red.

h] One durable and adorable tote.

i] Well-fitting sneaks. For both work-outs and hanging-outs!

j] One handsome all-weather, all-purpose coat. Make sure the buttons extend to at least three inches above your knee. And it's extra helpful if the coat has a removable lining so it's seasonless!

k] One signature, amazingly cool item which you love, love, love, LOVE – and get known for wearing! It becomes A CLASSIC YOU!

MIX 'N MATCH

Now that you're done taking these six **HOL-LYWOOD SCREEN TESTS,** you should be more aware of who you are from the inside out. I'm curious if you found out anything new about yourself. Were you surprised to discover a new passion, new goal, new belief, new quirk, new pet peeve? I invite you to share these six **HOLLYWOOD SCREEN TESTS** with friends and family members – and explore how well you really know the people you THINK you know.

As I mentioned at the start of this chapter, I'm sure you relate to more than one movie star icon. However, I am also sure that one movie star icon in particular wound up standing out as the starring-role player in your life – while one or two of the others tended to play co-starring roles.

I know I personally feel as if I'm half Fashionista and half Ingénue – most of the time. Although some days I feel 75% Ingénue with 25% Fashionista. Or 85% Fashionista with 15% Ingénue.

A fabulous idea is to check in with yourself first thing in the morning – or before you're dressing for an event. Sit in a relaxed position on your bed. Breathe in and out. Take some quiet time to tap into your **INTU-ITION**, so you can get a full sense for which

JAYE:

[50% INGÉNUE]

[50% FASHIONISTA]

DANA, my sister:

[10% ROCK-N-ROLLER]

[40% FASHIONISTA]

[50% SIRENISTA]

of these movie star icons is surfacing most within you for that day's or night's adventure.

For example, when I first met my soulmate, I could feel a little extra Sirenista rising within me before heading out to dinner with him. With this in mind, I instinctively wanted to add a little more Sirenista into my evening's ensemble. It felt right – so I went with it.

I definitely suggest you **always** take a meditative moment before you throw on your clothes for whatever outings you're heading toward. Use the insights you've gained from taking these **HOLLYWOOD SCREEN TESTS** and merge them with that day's specific intuitions!

Coming up ahead I will be offering some fun suggestions for how to dress for various outings. When you read my fashion tips, start with the movie star icon you most related to – your starring-role icon – and gather any tips which speak most personally to you. Next, read your co-starring icon's fashion tips. Again, choose the style ideas which you feel best suit you. Finally, browse through all the various movie star icon fashion ideas – as chances are there's a little something which will inspire you in each of these different, fabulous movie star icons! **Have fun! Happy fashion tip shopping!**

KAREN, my writer:

[10% SIRENISTA]

[40% BOHEMIAN PRINCESS]

[50% YOGANISTA]

MINDY, my other sister:

[70% FASHIONISTA]

[30%INGENUE]

HOLLYWOOD
[PLACES]
INTUITION

When a movie star walks into a restaurant – or a café – or a playground – their star quality can quickly steal the scene. In this **PLACES** section I will be offering tips to help you steal the scene wherever you go. After all, if you're wearing the right outfit to the wrong place – it will swiftly become the wrong outfit entirely – and you will thereby make the wrong impression on people. Remember that old Dr. John song? Well – you do NOT want to sing it to yourself like this...

I been in the right place
But it must have been the wrong shirt
I thought I said the right thing
But I must have worn a dumb skirt
I been in the right trip
But I must have worn inappropriate shoes
My hair was in a bad place
Now I feel I looked like bad news

No worries. Coming up, I will give you celebrity-insider tips which ensure that whenever you head out into the world, you will always be confidently wearing the absolutely perfect outfit for any place – so you will NEVER feel out of place.

Now that you've taken the **HOLLYWOOD SCREEN TEST**, you know a bit more about the starring and co-starring roles you want

to play when you're out and about. This section is set up so you can easily and quickly read up on specific style tips to help you for the roles you most want to play. However, after you're done reading your fashion tailored tips, do browse through the rest of the tips. Hey, you never know when an Ingénue can garner some good fashion advice from a Sirenista – and "advice versa"!

Also, just as a celebrity knows when they have a "hit movie" by the surplus of positive reviews they receive, you will know when you've hit upon a "hit outfit" by the amount of OOOOOH'S and AAAAAAAH'S and WHERE DID YOU GET THAT? you receive. Remember these outfits as your "go-to" outfits for the next time you feel as if you have nothing to wear!

If you're heading out in a weary mood, always pick something which makes you smile. It could be a tee-shirt with a feisty saying on it, red shoes, or your grandmother's sweater. Also, fragrance has a way of lifting one's mood. Or if you're always wearing jeans, switch it up with a casual dress and boots. **You'll immediately feel all dressed up with somewhere to go!**

STARCUPS RUN

When a celeb's running out for coffee, she never wants to look like she's trying too hard. Just as you can overly produce a movie, you can overly produce an outfit! Accessories are your loyal buddies. They'll fit you no matter how many calorie-laden Carameluccinos you down.

FASHIONISTA

So many clothes, so little time. If you're not a morning person, and need your coffee fix to operate your fashion instincts at your highest alpha levels, you should pick out what you want to wear the night before. I also recommend bringing a bag which has easy access to your cash, so you don't keep those Caffeinistas waiting too long in line behind you while you pay. Also keep in mind that it is hard to grab your precious coffee-to-go cup while holding a clutch purse – so consider bringing a bag which you can wear cross-body.

INGÉNUE

You usually wake up feeling pretty perky even before your coffee. Indeed you're as perky as your favorite freshly ironed, crisp, button-down shirt – which looks fabulous teamed up with your favorite jeans – with a long gorgeous scarf slipped through your jeans' belt loops to show off your adorable waistline. Or you can use this scarf to cinch in one of your fave oversized baby-doll tops that works with those jeans. Also remember: An organized handbag equals an organized day. You can handle any problem, when you're armed with an efficient handbag.

BOHEMIAN PRINCESS

Going out for coffee first thing in the morning after a fun evening of wine, men, and song? No time for concealer and mascara? Just leave on your shades. Sunglasses are also the perfect accessory to hide a multitude of secrets – a breakup, a bad facial, a sleepless night and an early wake-up call. Also, pull the scarf down from over your mouth and give yourself some air – breathe in the beautiful new day. Oh – and trim the bottoms of your jeans if they are frayed so badly that they get caught in your shoes. The last thing you want is to drag around coffee spills on your hem. One more goodie tip. If you have a particularly gorgeous bag, put a magazine inside – but not to read. Spread the magazine down on the ground to protect the bottom of your bag from your café's sticky spilled milk and coffee.

SIRENISTA

The regulars at your coffee place aren't simply there for the energizing effects of the coffee – but the energizing effects you have on them when you walk through the door! You love to turn heads – and can often feel those eyes looking at you from behind. With those long lines at many cafés the peeps behind you will have plenty of time to peep at your behind. I like to remind my sexiest celeb clients to always take a double look at your backside before you leave the house. If you are always tucking that blouse back in your bottoms, try a body suit. They help you to get that smooth look under fitted pants and skirts.

YOGANISTA

If you are heading directly to your local café right after taking a yoga class, recognize that there is no excuse not to look as gorgeous on your outside as you now feel inside. Be sure to leave your home prepared with a well-stocked, eco-friendly tote bag. Throw into this tote a new tee you can wear atop your yoga clothes to camouflage your sweat. Take your elastics out of your hair and put them on your wrist as a colorful bracelet. If you didn't have time to shower, put on some pretty perfume (and at least wash those pits!). Also – don't let a long line undo all the good be-ing you're ready to be. As you wait in line, think thoughts of gratitude for who you love and what you have. I know personally, everyday I wake up and say to myself: "Today I will do it better than I did yesterday."

ROCK-N-ROLLER

Make sure wherever you get dressed in the morning has lots of good light – or you might wind up wearing clashing clothes or dirty clothes or rumpled clothes. Your best go-to café look: coffee, tees, and you! Wear a tee with either jeans or a long skirt. Either way, I also suggest wearing extra high boots that have secret outside pockets to store your cash – which will then make it easier to grab that cup of joe and jump back on your wheels. Team up your look with a fantastic cycle jacket that has a fun expression or cool painted picture on its back – and be ready for your jacket to start up a conversation with the person in line behind you, so the time will pass quickly even if the line doesn't!

PLAYGROUND RUN

Save your money for your kid's college education. Fabulous style doesn't have to cost a lot of money. Keep it real and practical. Even if you already own and love the pricey stuff, ask yourself: Do you really want your Jimmy Choo's filled with sandbox sand?

PLAYGROUND RUN

BOHEMIAN PRINCESS

Are you petite? If so, you can shop for playful clothes at petite prices in the kids' department when you shop for your own kid(s). If you are anywhere from a size 0 to 6 in adults sizes you can match yourself up with any size from 10 to 14 in the tweens department. Ditto for snagging groovy kid's jewelry and watches in the tween department. Another fashion idea: Playgrounds are great for sporting your latest vintage tee with your guy's jeans. Be sure to wear a belt to hold those jeans upwardly mobile! Throw on colorful sneakers to satisfy both the fun and function factors.

INGÉNUE
Gee, I know you hate to get dirty, so let's be practical here and save those white pants and silky tops for the beach club. Also, let's make sure your pants are cropped – and no cuffs. Can you just imagine tracking hidden sand inside your cuffs onto your white, fluffy Flokati rug? I don't think so! No need to use a traditional diaper bag. Find a gorgeous oversized bag that can quickly adjust into an over-the-body hanging bag – so you can keep your hands über-free – especially handy if you are toting a toddler. Plus, be sure to fill this big bag with lots of fun, colorful, small zip bags to store snacks for your kids, and must-haves for every fashion emergency – or any emergency.

YOGANISTA

You are already dressed to play when you are in your favorite yoga clothes. Remember to keep it simple with your dangling crystal jewelry – so you can chase after your kid(s). Also, trade in your gym bag for a great belt bag to keep your hands free for swing-pushing. And be sure to pop one small ziplock bag filled with healthy nuts into your bag for you and your kid(s) to indulge in after you've worked up an appetite from all that swing-pushing!

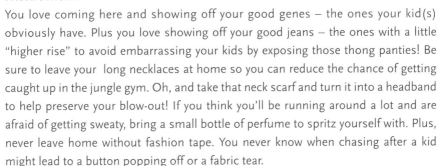

FASHIONISTA

You love coming here and showing off your good genes – the ones your kid(s) obviously have. Plus you love showing off your good jeans – the ones with a little "higher rise" to avoid embarrassing your kids by exposing those thong panties! Be sure to leave your long necklaces at home so you can reduce the chance of getting caught up in the jungle gym. Oh, and take that neck scarf and turn it into a headband to help preserve your blow-out! If you think you'll be running around a lot and are afraid of getting sweaty, bring a small bottle of perfume to spritz yourself with. Plus, never leave home without fashion tape. You never know when chasing after a kid might lead to a button popping off or a fabric tear.

SIRENISTA

First of all, YES – those stunning high heels will get stuck in the grass, so don't even think about wearing them! And save that miniskirt for cocktail hour. A good style plan is a fitted tee with sexy jeans and (gasp!) low heeled boots or even pretty colored sneakers. And if your jeans are on the long side since you're now sporting lower heels, definitely be sure to fold them into perfectly cropped capris. How? Fold up one hem approximately one to two inches, then pull the bottom of the jeans tight at ankle, to one side, until they are easily able to then be folded together and roll-hemmed up – until they are even and above sandbox level. If you need to use black fashion tape, definitely do!

ROCK-N-ROLLER

Ahhhhh, the joy of jungle gyms and swings and merry-go-rounds! You are at home here, letting loose and playing with your little ones. Put on your favorite flannel shirt and ripped up jeans with a low heeled boot. And be sure to slip those knuckle rings into your belt bag so you can catch that Frisbee with ease! And yes you can ditch the corny diaper bag and carry an oversized bag which expresses your feisty self. Bring two iPods. One for you to listen to your favorite tunes; the second for your kid(s) to listen to children's eBooks – in case your kid(s) suddenly starts to cry and doesn't want to play. Play them a happy eBook story and they will be back to wanting to happily play on that merry-go-round – especially if you join them!

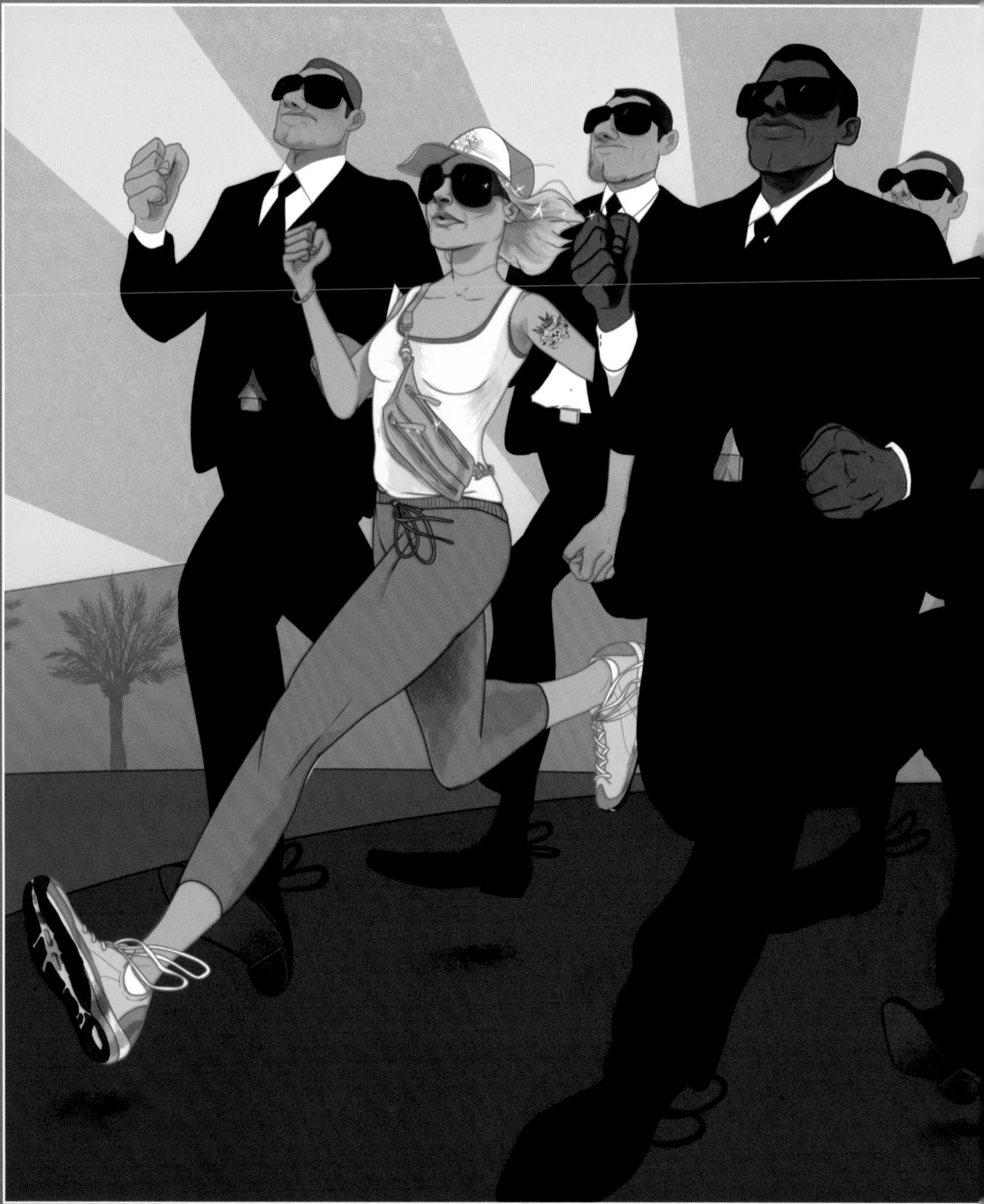

ACTUAL RUN

Always be sure to wear the right jog bra so you're not bouncing all over the place. My new favorite is one which has its own pocket for your iPod/phone! Genius! Invest in some good bottoms with a higher lycra count. They'll keep you "held in" better!

ACTUAL RUN

INGÉNUE

Ooooh, the thought of sweating in front of others is not a happy one. Be careful not to wear white tops and bottoms – as they tend to become see-through when you sweat. If you're worried about your hair getting messy, terry cloth headbands are not just for tennis players. You can find a great selection of these at any sporting goods store. If you wear them in combo with a high ponytail, you can help a blow-dry last a few days longer.

BOHEMIAN PRINCESS

It doesn't matter what kind of exercise you love to do to get in shape. Every kind of sports clothing which is out there, is ripe plucking for your shopping. You can mix biker shorts with a dancer's leotard. Or a tennis top with yoga pants. Or a golfer's top with a dancer's leggings. Scuba diving shops offer super fun tees which bring color and excitement to that pair of traditional grey sweat pants you've owned since high school. Buy good sneakers which fit your feet properly – instead of being suckered into buying those cute sneaks. If you want cutesy in your sneaks, you can always buy colorful laces to pump up their fun volume.

ROCK-N-ROLLER

You not only love to listen to rock – you love for your body to be toned and hard like a rock. Your journey to getting to be a rock-hard rocker should be a fearless and fiercely dressed one. I recommend having fun wearing layers on top of layers of different colored tanks – and jog bras. Also include some tie-dyed wife beaters layered in. For badass bottoms, consider wearing boxer shorts and ripped fishnets with your sneakers. Another cool look is sweatpants cut into boxer short length– with or without leggings beneath...And If you're working out as well as running, fuggetabout those silly, sand-filled, pastel-colored free weights. Bring props like bricks and cinder blocks to the park. Obviously bring your iPod – loaded up with your favorite body-movement inspiring tunes and lose yourself in the music. Pretty soon your body will be as ripped as your jeans and fishnets.

FASHIONISTA

The good news about running: it will give you extra energy for shopping! More good news: there are many cute outfits you can wear to do your running. In fact, much of today's workout gear is so cool looking you will be tempted to wear it even when you're not in training. Some of today's workout tops look adorable with jeans. When working out, play it smart with the jewelry. No dangly earrings which can get caught in your iPod or lost on the running track. Be sure to wear waterproof eyeliner and mascara – and bring a small mirror with you to make sure that even though you are running your makeup is not.

YOGANISTA

It's a known principle that when doing yoga it helps to see your body, so you know truthfully how you're moving. The more naked the body, the easier it is to judge if you have proper alignment. So much so, there are now many naked yoga classes. If you feel proud of your yoga-toned body, by all means feel free to don a tight-fitting yoga top and lycra leggings to work out in. The goal: Your workout clothes should cling to you but not overly bind you. Remember: the darker you wear, the slimmer your look. If you're doing actual yoga do not wear a too-loose tee, because you wont be able to do headstands or many of the maneuvers which require twisting and speed.

SIRENISTA
You love being chased after by handsome men – and so you know you have to do some running to be chase-worthy. As far your being chaste – well, that's another NC-17 story. Of course you want to be dressed to the nines so you look like a Ten while you are running – yet you want to be practical too. What's a Sirenista to do? First things first: put those "girls" in the right jogging bra. Happy days: you can buy a jogging bra which fits so well it actually works like a Wonderbra. Another trick of the boob trade: Buy one size smaller so the "girls" get an extra boost being squished inside. Also, if you're wearing fitted leggings, watch out for V.P.L. (Visible Panty Lines). Wear a clip on bag to carry your cellphone – so if your crush calls, you can be sure to answer in a highly breathy voice and tell him how sweaty you are.

WEIGHT CENTER RUN

Keep the colors you wear monochromatic. It's definitely more slimming and easier to get dressed in a rush if you stay with solid, neutral colors. It's common knowledge that black is the most slimming color of 'em all!

WEIGHT CENTER RUN

FASHIONISTA

Just because you gained weight, it is NOT an excuse to gain an entirely new wardrobe. Save your money. If you invest too much in new bigger sizes then you are telling your subconscious (and conscious!) that you plan to remain this bigger size. Search in your present Fashionista wardrobe for long flowy skirts and great lightweight tees. A good dieting inspiration: Shop for new gorgeous bathing suits to wear once you lose the weight. Wear these suits instead of undies to remind you daily of your goal. In general, wear your favorite darker colored clothes, and distract from your weight gain with stunning accessories. Indeed groovy accessories and shoes always fit – no matter your weight. As for shoes...If you're doing a weigh in, wear easy to remove sling backs or zip off boots. If you're feeling down because your scale is high, pamper thyself with a mani/pedi!

BOHEMIAN PRINCESS

You love vintage finds – like unusual shawls. Now's the time to swathe yourself in a one-of-a-kind wrap. If you're going to mix patterned fabrics, find ones with vertical lines or teeny tiny flowers. Know: Big flower prints make you look bigger. Also, bigger bags will make you look smaller – and smaller bags will make you look bigger.

YOGANISTA

Good news! Your pretty yoga lycra pants are slenderizing on the thighs and tush. Plus, if you wear them during the day you will "be more conscious of your body" – and thereby less tempted to eat badly. If you feel a little too conscious sporting lycra in public, throw on a pretty light weight dress over your lycra leggings. If you're wearing a fun yoga tank top, make sure your bra straps don't show. The miracle of double stick tape can instantly convert a standard bra into a razorback bra in minutes. Tape together the back of the bra straps so they meet and greet. Tempted to eat something yummy? Replace saying: "Yummmm" with "Ommmmm." Become conscious of the vibration in your throat. Still your mind from anxiety, and you will have more discipline to still your mouth from chewing every yummy thing in sight.

ROCK-N-ROLLER

You might love heavy metal – but you don't love feeling heavy when listening to heavy metal. Thankfully you already own lots of black in your wardrobe – the best slenderizing color since the beginning of time. Indeed for you "B.C." stands for Black Clothes. Keep away from black leather as it creates the illusion of poundage. If you're proud of specific tattoos, draw attention to them and away from weight gain. If you gained weight in your belly, do not wear midriffs! Wear a loose tee with your favorite chain belt, creating a rocking rocker's tunic.

SIRENISTA

You're a big fan of Mae West's line: "I generally avoid temptation...unless I can't resist it." You love Mae's curves too – but sometimes when you're a little too tempted by those carbs you worry you've made your curvy bod' a little less tempting. Don't fret! Put on your highest heels for instant slenderization. Make them stunning stilettos and nobody will notice an extra ounce on you. Also: Accentuate a positive body part to distract from a negative body part. And, play with cosmetics in a new way to jump-start your sexual/sensual confidence. Buy a new red lipstick or a glittery shadow. NEVER allow yourself to dress in slovenly loose clothes because you feel fat. Remember: Sirenista is an attitude. Be it. Dress it. Then be it even more! As Mae West said: "It isn't what I do, but how I do it. It isn't what I say, but how I say it, and how I look when I do it and say it." If you continue to dress the part of Sirenista you will ALWAYS remain the fab Sirenista you are – and remain a temptation no man can resist!

INGÉNUE

Now is the perfect time to wear that yummy, light-weight cashmere cardigan set. It's classy and slenderizing. Also, wear loose fitting chinos or pretty pinstripe pants topped off with a crisply ironed button-down shirt. A suit makes you appear slimmer – but only if the jacket is fitted and the pants are straight-legged. Choose solid and darker colors then add favorite accessories like pearls. Play around with scarves. My favorite way to wear a scarf: Fold the scarf in half. Fold the scarf around your neck. Make a knot with both ends. Or put on the scarf backwards and wrap the scarf around your neck back to forwards.

FIRST DATE

A little black dress is a good universal first date option – as long as you pick one which fits you well. You gotta make sure you're fitting pretty!

FIRST DATE

INGÉNUE

This is your favorite role, so you are ready for those lights, camera, action. But of course not too much action – as you are a sweet Ingénue! Your goal: For this to be your LAST first date ever! As your own personal dresser, I would right now be adorning you in your flirtiest little dress – one which is just short enough to show off those fabulous gams. And I'd advise you to bring a wrap J.I.C. (just in case). After all you never know if you're going for a moonlit walk which will lead you to that unforgettable moonlit first kiss. Which reminds me: Wear sensible heels! Also wear your fave strand of pearls. Your look: Classic, classy, demure, timeless!

FASHIONISTA

If you want to be irresistible (duh) then you must resist mixing too many "of the moment" looks all at one time. You will wind up looking like you are hiding the real you behind those bows, bangles, and beads – or simply trying too hard. Basically, too much of a trendy thing is always a nauseous thing. Pick one style statement and stick with it. Whatever you wear, make sure the size fits you. If it doesn't, pay a tailor to make sure it does. It's always better to wear a simple something which is tailored to your body, than a trendy something which doesn't fit you well at all.

SIRENISTA

Celebrities know it's called SHOW BUSINESS – not SHOW TOO MUCH BUSINESS. Dress with an R rating – not NC-17. You want to watch out for THE SEXUAL INTIMIDATION FACTOR. Your goal: Offer FIRST DATE BAIT – so he senses what is to come if he comes back for more – and more. I love a wrap dress for a first date. You can adjust it to the amount of skin exposure you prefer. Also a flattering top with your most butt-friendly jeans and killer heels can give you that "sexy-without-trying" vibe. Also: Pick soft touchable fabrics – like silk or cashmere – to lure your date to want to touch you – even if you're not that kind of girl – at least not on the FIRST date! Load up on bangles. I love the sexy sound the clinking together makes. Keep in mind your date's height before you wear your highest heeled shoes.

YOGANISTA

Be true to your casual style – but NO workout clothes or hoodies or hair up in ponytails! Slip on a favorite top with a great skirt and pile on a layer of necklaces. BUT – do NOT fidget too much with those necklaces! Consider wearing a simple little black dress – which you can use as a little black canvas – and let your accessories take center stage.

BOHEMIAN PRINCESS

Show up as any good princess would – looking like a gal any guy would feel lucky to put high on his pedestal. This means that you should wear a sexy dress which shows off your shape – and save jeans with the ripped and see through back pockets for the second or third date. You could also wear your fave flowy top – to give some mystery as to what lies beneath. If the top's sheer, allow your bra straps to show ONLY if they are silky, lacy, or colorful. Or let a not-so-innocent camisole peek through. If you're wearing a sheer top, avoid creating a huge bulge from your vintage belt buckle by tucking in your shirt, or leaving off the belt. Instead lace a piece of narrow elastic through your belt loops to keep your pants up and achieve smooth lines with no red indentations in your belly button from that heavy buckle.

ROCK-N-ROLLER

You still want to feel femme so hold off on the head-to-toe, full black leather and Metallica look. You don't want to scare him off right from the start by looking like you're auditioning for Grease. If he's going to be afraid of you it's 100% gonna be because he's falling for your charisma, talent, beauty, and brains. Lure him in by dangling what you got – not shoving it in his face. Meaning? Whatever your rocker look, enhance it with one thing lacy or feminine. Wear a peek-a-boo black lace camisole beneath a tank top or low necked sweater. Wear feminine, lace stockings – instead of torn fishnets – beneath your skirt or dress. Wear a colorful silk scarf with your black bomber jacket. Wear a long piece of lace fabric strung through your belt loops. Wear bling-enhanced butterfly barrettes to hold your hair away from your pretty face.

LAST DATE

Go through your checklist of everything he ever told you he liked to see you in. The perfect exit outfit would be something he bought for you – especially if it was something you both picked out together.

LAST DATE

ROCK-N-ROLLER

What did he say was his favorite outfit on you? Bring it on. This is your [PHOTO-GRAPHIC MEMORY OPP!] Winner style concept: A lacy or satin camisole or tank, beneath a soft old sweater, worn with your sexiest skirt, fishnets, and boots! Or wear your sexiest ripped-up jeans with a cami/tank slipped under a tee. Choose a cami/tank which has lots of lycra. If worn correctly this miracle accessory can rid you of Dunlop Disease (when your tummy done lop over your pants)! Pick a cami/tank that's a little longer – then tuck it into your jeans and there will no trace of the "girdle" you're sportin'. Also, boyfriend panties under baggy jeans are a sexy look for saying adios to that no-good boyfriend. What WERE you thinking?

SIRENISTA

Nothing says sexy like a woman who is comfortable in her own skin – or comfy in leopard skin! Tonight consider wearing animal prints – so you can leave a lasting print on his heart! Dress in a few extra layers – a shawl and a sweater – so throughout the night you can keep seductively removing one piece at a time – until you do the final removal – this unworthy man from your life! Oh – and spray an extra layer of fragrance on yourself – so your scent stays on him (and his sheets, etc.) long after you've slammed that door shut.

YOGANISTA

What's your best body part? Highlight it – and consider your fab non-obvious body parts. For example, gorgeously rounded shoulders can be just as sexy as cleavage – especially if showing them off in itty bitty spaghetti straps. If your back is strong, wear a halter. If your collarbones are stand-outs, wear a pretty choker. Are your calves nicely carved? Wear a skirt and fab shoes. Pick touchable fabrics – but you be the chooser of how much he can touch you! Although you might not want to make up with this guy, DO make up your face – even if you never wear cosmetics. Put on a good moisturizer and foundation. Try a little smoky colored Kohl liner – but keep the glitter for the lip gloss.

FASHIONISTA

Leave the guy with a K.I.S.S. (Keep It Simple Stupid). Don't dress like you're trying too hard to make him want you. If you hold a stereotyped belief that the more "racy 'n lacy" the sexier – turn down that stereotyping music. I have seen many a man swoon for the lady who is wearing a simple, slightly-low cut black top, butt-hugging jeans, and stilettos. Make sure those high heels do NOT fit so tightly that your toes look like little hot dog sausages. And remember – a pair in a relationship is like a pair of shoes. If the pair is hurting too much – toss this pair aside. There's always a better fitting pair out there!

INGÉNUE

Dress "accidentally sexy" – so your guy feels you're very "whatevah!" about the break up. How? Try a button-down shirt fitted to the extreme – but not too extreme. Shop for a shirt where the buttons begin to pucker – then buy one size bigger. Show him just a whisper of that hollow between your breasts. Often that whisper speaks louder than the full cleavage shout-out. While you're sending mixed messages – create a fun mixed-metallic message by merging gold and silver bangle bracelets! As far as your bottom line – wear your favorite jeans or a cute denim skirt. No cheap panties! Even if he doesn't get to see them, you'll know you're wearing your finest panty ammo.

BOHEMIAN PRINCESS

Just because you and this dude were a bad match, doesn't mean your clothes should be. Tonight don't risk as much in your eclectic tastes. You don't want to give this guy any reason to say silently to himself, "That outfit is sooo wacky – and so I'm happy not to be with this wacky girl!" If you're going to mix 'n match, do it by merging sexy with conservative clothes. A great idea: **GIVE HIM THE PINK SLIP TO LET HIM KNOW HE'S FIRED FROM YOUR LOVE LIFE.** Wear a pink slip beneath a sweet light-weight vintage dress. You will laugh to yourself all night how you're giving him "the pink slip." After the break up, double-duty this slip as a dress. (Insider Info: Many a celeb has worn a well fitting silk slip on the red carpet!) Get your hair professionally blown – so you can toss those locks gloriously in his face as you walk out the door.

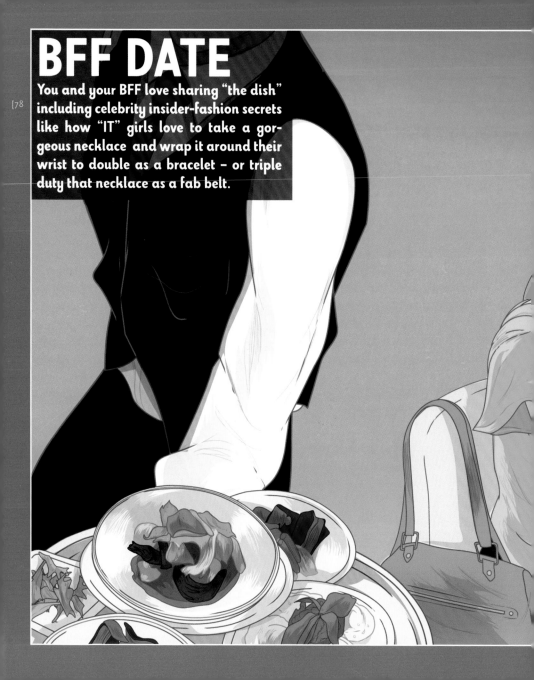

BFF DATE

You and your BFF love sharing "the dish" including celebrity insider-fashion secrets like how "IT" girls love to take a gorgeous necklace and wrap it around their wrist to double as a bracelet – or triple duty that necklace as a fab belt.

BFF DATE

BOHEMIAN PRINCESS

Often when you meet your BFF for a bite she wants to gobble up what you're wearing. You're known for making disparate styles look fabulous together. A good BFF Date Look: An unusually patterned vintage dress teamed with expensive Christian Louboutin boots and a groovy, inexpensive coat purchased at Target! You're also known for being good hearted and sharing – but be sure to remind/warn friends that your adventurous style is not best shared with everyone – although your friend can have some of your French fries! If you're wearing a layer of eclectic necklaces, you can sweetly give one to your BFF.

YOGANISTA
You love meeting friends for a bite after a good yoga class, so invest in fun bags to store spare clothes within. Buy organic cotton, colored bags which reverse from one color to another for double the wear. This duo-colored bag will fool friends into thinking you have extra bags – and save you money! If you want to save time too, invest in gorgeous tunics to throw on over your "yoga uniform." If you're planning to shop with your BFF, stay in yoga gear, so you can easily slip on clothes over it. Bring along pantyhose or spanx if you're shopping for dress-up clothes.

SIRENISTA

Your girlfriends look to you for "how to look like a femme fatale" fashion finds. So, even if you are having a low-key meet-up with a platonic pal, keep true to your seductress style. Wear a sexy tank top with comfy low-rise sweats or jeans. True friends know you feel happiest when decked out head-to-toe-ring – and they want you to be happy! So wear those sexy, strappy high heeled sandals with jeans! If it's cold, feel free to feel hot in your knee high boots! While we're talking girl talk, let's be honest. You never know if you will pick up some new sexy guy while out. Or if you'll do an impromptu, post-meal rendezvous! True Sirenistas plan ahead and ALWAYS wear their sexiest underwear!

INGÉNUE

The scarf is the perfect "cross-generational" Ingénue accessory – be you: a young hipster or classic lady who lunches. I recommend you throw on a scarf with just about everything. Try tying a fun printed scarf on your favorite handbag! Having a bad hair day? Wear a super fashionable, oversized floppy hat – which will also protect your face from the sun if you're eating outdoors. Sunglasses are also a girl's best friend when meeting your best friend in the great outdoors. Those big oversized-ones are perfect – as they are not only stylish but practical. Their wide sides also protect the sensitive skin around your eyes.

ROCK-N-ROLLER

If you were to tell your best friend that you loved her as much as your most beaten up jeans – that would be one helluva compliment. And your beat up/frayed-at-the-bottom jeans are the perfect complement for your slightly shrunken tee, for a BFF lunch or dinner date. If you don't already have a shrunken leather bomber jacket, here's a psssssssecret: You can buy adorable, mini leather jackets in the boy's department. If you decide to go shopping for one with your BFF, be efficient. Wear a fabulous knapsack so you can ditch your shopping bag, then jump on your bike and give your new duds and BFF the ride of their life back home.

FASHIONISTA

First of all "Faux diamonds = good!" But "Faux friends = bad!" You are loyal beyond belief. One of your favorite expressions: "A friend is someone who stabs you in the front." Your friends love how you tell them the truth – not only about their love life (the men to keep/not keep), but their fashion life (the outfits to keep/not keep). They think of you as their revered Fashion Cheerleader and Mistress of Reinvention. They are always curious to see what you show up wearing – as your hair is often in an entirely new style. And at past meals you've often shown up in a [FASHION FIRST]. You were the first to wear a headband – before the magazine's made them cool again. You were the first to merge your Mom's old gold charm bracelets with your new one. You were the first to wear knee-highs with Mary Janes with a short skirt – with a pair of mini bike shorts under that mini...of course

MEETING [WITHOUT A CASTING COUCH]

Employers use short-cuts to suss out who you are. Your clothes are always quickie cliff notes for analyzing who you are. You will always win over a future employer by dressing in a style they can relate to. Plus stick to classic colors like gray, black, navy, camel, and brown.

THE MALL STREET JOURNAL

INTERVIEW IN SESSION PLEASE BE QUIET

MEETING [WITHOUT A CASTING COUCH]

ROCK-N-ROLLER

The image you present when you first walk into that interview will speak louder than even your smartest interview answer. Although it might be hard – you gotta separate your groovy, social, party-girl self from your brilliant, professional self. Wearing black is totally fine – but no leather. Go light on that makeup. You're not auditioning for a rock band. And go light on that perfume. You're not a human room deodorizer. Also: No dark nail polish. No gum. No iPod. No sunglasses. No soda (because no belching!). No piercings jutting out. No inky tattoos showing. No crazy hair colors. No fishnets. No patterned hose. Check your helmet at reception – and be sure to smooth out any chin strap lines.

YOGANISTA

Kim Zoller from Image Dynamics says: "55% of another person's perception of you is based on how you look." Make sure whatever you wear has a little structure. Swap that hoodie for a blazer. Swap your lycra leggings for a pair of wide leg trousers. Do not wear tee shirts with Buddhist or political sayings on them. Even if you are aware that employees of an organization dress casually on the job, dress up anyway. This means no flip-flops or sneakers or Birkenstocks or clogs. And ditch that backpack and/or fanny pack.

SIRENISTA

Forget what some of those gals on <u>The Apprentice</u> and <u>Sex And The City</u> have worn. Your skirt should cover your thighs when you cross your legs. Do not show too much cleavage – and no free peep show at your bra straps or camisoles. Your personality and brilliance should take center stage not your body and ensemble. If you wind up being remembered for what you wore, then you wore the wrong thing. Plan ahead and stay away from silky shirts to avoid any embarrassing underarm stains. And although it's a jungle out there in the corporate world, no zebra or leopard print is allowed!

INGÉNUE

You are a good girl and eager to dress for success. Happily, this is where you can shine above the rest. You will always win over an employer by dressing in a sweet and classic suit in navy, black, camel, or gray. The skirt should be long enough to sit comfortably without worrying about pulling a Sharon Stone from *Basic Instinct*. If you want to slam-dunk your look, call the company's Human Resources office and directly ask what to wear. Or, visit the office with the excuse you want to pick up company info – then check out what employees wear. (Note: Make sure you don't spy on a casual Friday.) Arrive early for your interview, then check yourself out in the company's rest room mirror – to make sure your hair isn't sticking up à la Alfalfa from *The Little Rascals*. Oh – and get that headband off your hair and stash it in your matching navy, black, camel, or gray bag. Now go get 'em, tiger!

BOHEMIAN PRINCESS

Avoid wearing overly bright or large-patterned fabrics. It's best to wear a solid color for your pants/skirt/blazer (like navy, black, camel, or gray), then add a splash of color or small-patterned fabric for your shirt. Limit that jewelry to nothing too dangly and jangly – as you don't want to distract the interviewer from what you have to say – or even distract yourself! Also: Turn off that cellphone before the interview! If you think you'll be running around all day before your meeting (or even sitting a lot) pick a fabric which won't get rumpled before you arrive. Do a double check for any mothball odor before you leave the house.

FASHIONISTA

Don't confuse dressing for an interview with dressing for a social event. And you don't want to look like you spent all your pay on your interview look. You have plenty of time for that, after you get the gig. Pick out your outfit the night before and arrive to your meeting less frazzled. Imagine what the other person will see when you enter the room. Do you look approachable or entitled? Don't push the trendy-meter too far. Always err on the conservative side. If you've bought a new outfit, be sure to remove telltale tags and extra buttons – and cut off those zigzag threads which keep pocket slits closed! If your clothes are dry-clean, take them to the cleaners after an interview, so they are ready for your next interview – or your first day at your new job!

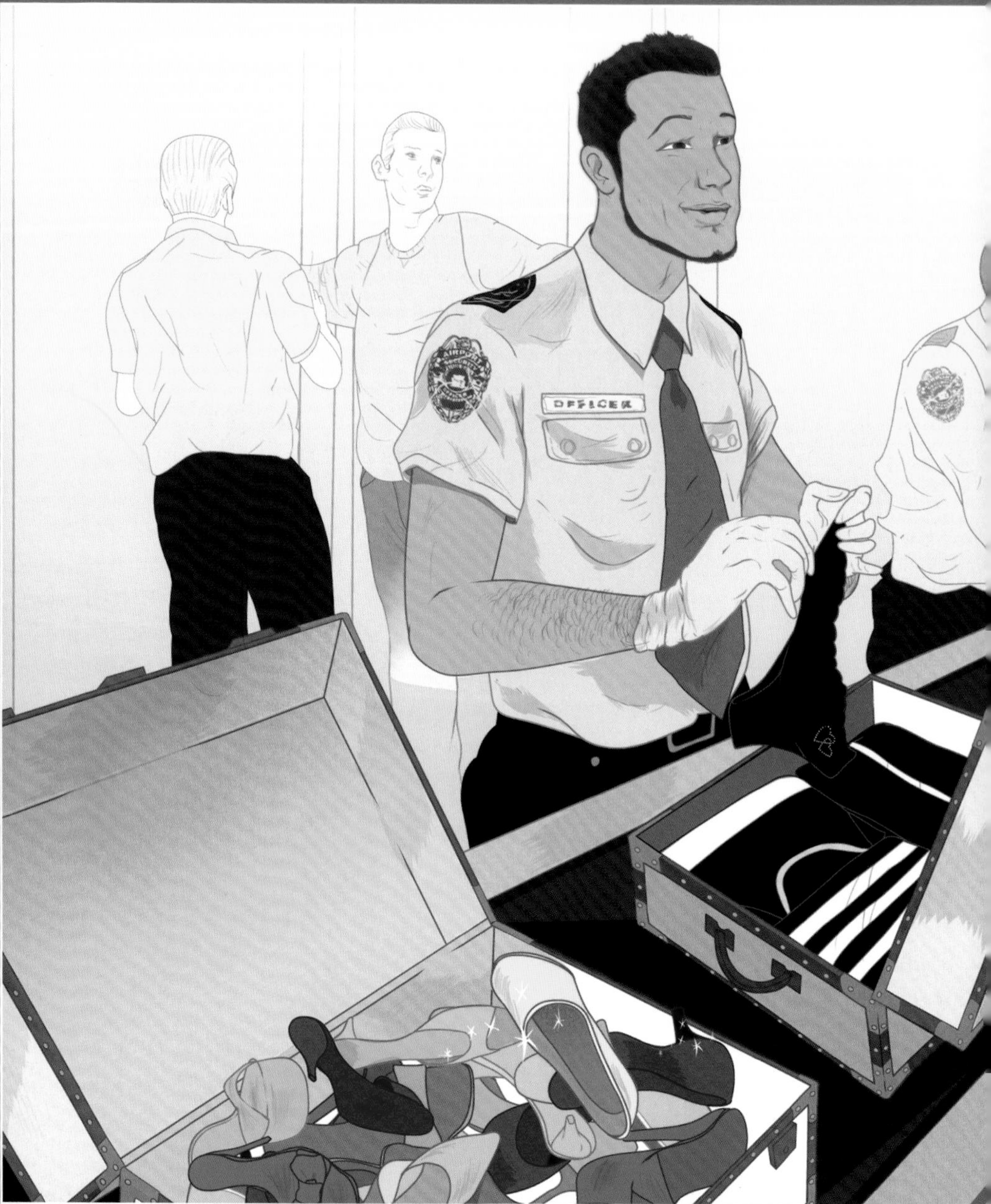
OFFICER

PLANES, TRAINS, AND LIMOUSINES

Look for fabrics with stretch so you won't stress out about the wrinkles. Pack with clothes which are in a complementary two-color theme, so you have more mix-n-match outfit choices.

PLANES, TRAINS, AND LIMOUSINES

SIRENISTA

They say, "enjoy the journey"! You can enjoy yours by dressing in your Sirenista best – keeping in mind the ever present, "you nevah know where you'll meet your future Mr. Sirenista" philosophy. Simultaneously, keep in mind "the cross your leg" rule. Can you sit for an extended time in what you're wearing and not arrive with whisker creases across your lap? Also keep in mind "Murphy's Law" about traffic delays. Wear flat shoes in case you must run for a gate. Pack stilettos in your small travel bag. If limo-ing, keep your knees together as you exit. Nobody needs to see your unmentionables – even if you paid a fortune for that lacy thong thing.

INGÉNUE

A good traveling outfit is a winkle-free-fabric skirt and top teamed with a cashmere sweater – all in the same color family – and all matching your packed pants and a no-fuss, wrap dress. Add on slip-offable shoes – but no belt. No need to set off metal detectors. Make sure your packed pants are hemmed to the right level for your pumps – which should be the same heel level that matches all the skirts and dresses you're traveling with. Travel expert Carolyn Paddock also suggests while on a plane you twist your hair into a high bun, so you can rest your head – not worrying about flattening your hairstyle. As soon as you arrive, let your hair down and it will have incredible body instantly! Also pack a compact mirror in your bag to check for makeup smears and peanut crumbs.

ROCK-N-ROLLER

Pack your favorite monochromatic black and gray clothes – including one nice, little black dress – which you can either play up as high-rent or down as low-rent – depending upon your accessories. Don't wear too much metal while traveling – or you'll take forever to pass through the metal detectors. Bring travel lint removers – as black clothes mega-attract dustiness and hair. Make sure your iPod is powered up – and that you did not forget your chargers. Watch it with the alcohol. It will dehydrate you. Drink at least eight oz. of water every hour.

BOHEMIAN PRINCESS

You can travel in wrinkle-free style by donning a flowy skirt or flowy pants and a pretty tee. Bring a vintage sweater – as planes get cold. Keep a few small bags inside your travel bag, filled with sample-size cosmetics and perfume. If you're wearing an eye-mask for sleep, bring an eye lash curler – as you might bend lashes with the mask. Meanwhile, back inside your big suitcase, you can stop wrinkles from happening by laying two pieces of clothes flat – then wrapping them into each other, creating a cushiony effect. Always keep a second name and address label inside your suitcase – just in case your luggage gets lost, and the outside label comes off.

FASHIONISTA

I know you hate NOT having LOTS of clothing options, but you have to pack light. Pick basics: 1 pair of pants, 1 skirt, 1 shirt – all of which mix-n-match. Keep it interesting with fun accessories. Pack clothes in reverse chronological order than you plan on wearing them – so you save time scrounging for what you need when you arrive. Tie an old colorful scarf on your bag as a marker – so yours stands out in the conveyor belt crowd. Pack a scarf for your hair, in case it gets messed in transit. Bring a big carry-on vinyl or shiny patent leather bag – which you can wipe clean if it gets dirty. Watch it with that perfume – as a courtesy to the person sitting beside you. Ditto on bringing mints/breath spray.

YOGANISTA

Yoga clothes are fabulous for traveling – so you can run for that gate – and absorb whatever sweat happens. Wear slip-offable cloth shoes – and nobody behind you in line will wish bad karma upon you. But don't wear flip flops – as they are difficult to run in if you're running late. Bring a groovy, zipper-a-plenty knapsack as the perfect travel bag companion. Stuff it with one wardrobe change, mints, book, a small moisturizer – and all your travel identification. Which reminds me to remind you: Keep all your jewelry, keys, medication, traveller's checks, and credit cards packed in this carry-on. As for your big suitcase, cut down on wrinkles by folding clothes in the same way stores do. As for worry-wrinkles, do this yoga-esque exercise: Pinch flesh between thumb and pointer finger with your opposite thumb and pointer finger. Massage gently.

RED CARPET

If you're going to get a facial or eyebrow/lip waxing for the big event, be sure to do it at least five days before – in case you break out in a rash. Ditto for a haircut faux pas – give yourself five days wiggle room to get hair extensions or a second trim.

RED CARPET

INGÉNUE

I know you want to play it safe – but I encourage you to stretch a little outside your comfort zone – maybe with a fabric which is a wee bit stretchy to show off your hard work at the gym. White and neutral colored dresses are always elegant hues – unless you're dressing up for a wedding – then NEVER wear white, as it competes with the bride. If it's a daytime affair, avoid black. Opera-length gloves are very Audrey Hepburn gorgeous – but be sure to only wear them with sleeveless or strapless dresses. A classic yet sexy look – which succeeds on nearly all body types – is a cowl neck in the front of the dress. Ditto on a dress with a cowl neck in the back – to show off a sexy back. Also consider wearing your hair up, then sporting dramatic sparkly earrings.

ROCK-N-ROLLER

My number one recommended Rocker-at-Formal-Event-Look is a gorgeous black dress and a little faux fur – or a real fur – stole wrap. If you go for fishnets, make sure your dress' fabric is not clingy. The last thing you want is to stand up and look like you reeled in the catch of the day with your gown. Be sure to rock out only one sexy feature: tattoos, boobs, gams, or tush. And do NOT think that a formal event is an opportunity to wear lots of chains and/or bold jewelry. Wear only one "Rocker Girl Signature Piece." Glittery eyeshadow is allowed – but only if you promise NOT to wear dark lipstick. Let your eyes be your dramatic stand-out act!

SIRENISTA

I have one word for you to create a sexy, yet elegant look for a formal event: COLOR! Find a sleek, classy dress which is red, hot pink, purple, or turquoise – pick your most favorite or lucky (or get-lucky!) color. If it's daytime event, avoid sequined fabrics. A good classy, yet vixen-like cut: a dramatic one-shoulder dress. If the ensemble requires a belt, add a very thin rhinestone one. If you're a bit curvy, let the belt rest on hips – not above. You also can "sex it up" with shoes. Choose strappy stilettos – maybe with some sparkly rhinestones!

BOHEMIAN PRINCESS

Now is the time to go shopping for that one-of-a-kind vintage item – so you really stand out in the crowd! Make sure the item not only shows off your terrific shape – but is itself in terrific shape! Avoid wearing anything fraying-at-the-edges or stained. If something is a bit too loose, take it to the dressmaker. If something is a bit too tight, consider wearing a gorgeous vintage corset – and create a sexy hourglass shape. (Just make sure you can breathe and eat and laugh and sneeze!) Mix and match your dress with modern touches by adding in indie-designer jewelry, shoes, and bag.

FASHIONISTA

This is your favorite, most-fun dress-up time! I recommend you try a sexy little number which is one of these numbers: [1] backless, [2] strapless, [3] deep low front or [4] slit up the leg. Work it baby and be ready to stick out in the crowd! Just make sure your body parts are not excessively sticking out! This means watch those boobies – and no bra straps showing. Keep accessories to a minimum. Make it all about [THE DRESS]. Bring a roll of fashion emergency duct tape. I have used this wonder-secret tape on everything from the back of my sling-backs, to my heels, to the stop-the-strap-slip-factor.

YOGANISTA

Here is your chance to show off that buff yoganista bod. If you have fab arms, highlight them. Ditto on those especially carved calves. If bling is not your thing, go for a great matte fabric – or sparkly gold colored fabric – which hugs your body. Complement it all with a fab fringe-trimmed wrap. Remember, if you're wearing open toe shoes to put on pretty toe-nail polish. And NO fabric shoes or sneakers. Only Jerry Seinfeld can get away with wearing those to a big event. If you're not used to wearing high heels, practice wearing them for a couple of days around the house. If there will be dancing at the event, don't just walk in them, salsa in them – on both floors and carpets. If you know there will be lots of stairs, practice walking down the stairs in them.

HOLLYWOOD

INTUITION

There's a famous principle called the Pareto Principle. It's an 80/20 rule – which applies to oh so many things – and says 20% of your effort/attention leads to 80% of your results/enjoyment. For example...

The Pareto Principle

20% of married peeps account for 80% of divorces

20% of your carpet gets 80% of the wear

20% of streets account for 80% of the traffic

20% of criminals account for 80% of crime

20% of motorists account for 80% of accidents

And finally, yes, it applies to a woman's wardrobe...**20% of the clothes/accessories in your closet are worn 80% of the time.**

How can you benefit from becoming aware of the Pareto Principle? You can become more consciously discerning when shopping for new things. It's good to keep asking yourself when confronted with a THING you THINK you need:

IS THIS A WANT HAVE?
IS THIS A MUST HAVE?
IS THIS A LUST HAVE?

Ahem – the LUST HAVE category is the one which winds up covering the 20% you wear most of them time! With this in mind it would be a wonderful goal to try to change your **Clothing and Accessories Pareto Principle**

so you wind up wearing 80% of what you own – by carefully purchasing mostly LUST HAVEs – things you know you will really love and appreciate. Which brings me to another important philosophy of mine:

Jaye-ism
[**Do not to be suckered in by a sale or you will wind up with a closet full of dud clothes and accessories you never wear.**]

Coming up ahead I've listed the ten main categories of things you must be sure to own – things which will absolutely spiff up your style from drab to fab.

As I've confessed many times already, I am a big fan of accessories. They're a fun way to keep giving your existing wardrobe "personality makeovers" with just the click of a bracelet closing or the swoosh of a scarf being tied.

If you're starting to get bored by your accessories – don't toss them – repurpose them. You can reuse a necklace as a purse strap. You can decorate the toes of a pair of pumps with earrings. You can sew old earrings or old beaded necklaces onto the pockets of your jeans. You can sew a gorgeous bracelet onto the end of a scarf to serve as a buckle, thereby creating a very cool belt. **Get imaginative.**

Hat too big? Purchase foam
weatherstripping tape and use
on inner brim to fill it out.

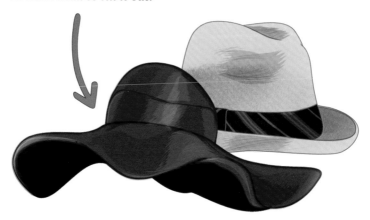

[HATS]

Can you say "Paparazzi-Proof?" The bigger the brim the better! My celeb insider secret: Find a foldable, crushproof hat that can easily roll up, then always keep in your IT bag. Use it to keep your "one more day 'til hair is colored" look an under-the-hat-secret. Grab a few girlfriends and go hat shopping together! It's great gal pal bonding. Make sure your back view in the hat looks as good as your front view. **A tilted hat to one side creates a face-slimming effect. A hat with a small, close brim is flattering for a narrow face.** A cute pillbox hat is a great height-creator, and thereby flattering for round or wide faces. If a hat is too big, purchase foam weatherstripping tape – which is sticky on one side and soft/cushy on the other. Stick it inside the hat around the inner brim to fill it out a bit. Three Fun "Must-Hat" Classics: a newsboy cap, a fedora, and a big oversized sunhat for the beach – to keep your lovely skin younger, longer!

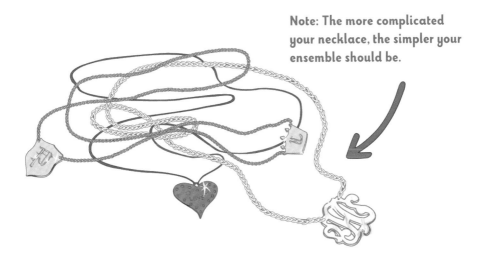

Note: The more complicated your necklace, the simpler your ensemble should be.

[NECKLACES]

You can always tell what mood a celeb is in by the necklace she's wearing. For example: If it's a name plate, she's saying "Yo! Don't forget who I am!" If it's a heart, she's in a happy relationship. If it's a baby, the stork is a-coming. If it's pearls she's letting you know she's in a Hollywood Classic Ingénue kinda mood. As far as insider tips – a great celeb secret is to buy diamonds by the yard. The faux kind are my fave. They add a sparkle to your neck even from across the room. Sometimes if a star is not feeling her best she will put extra attention on her jewels hoping nobody will notice she's in a funk – and hoping that wearing something sparkly might make her feel a bit more sparkly. As mentioned earlier, I love layer-

[BAGS]

A simultaneously gorgeous and practical bag is always the IT item. For me the perfect bag incorporates ...

1] LIGHT WEIGHT: I hate when my bag is so heavy that I end up with red strap marks that dig into the same exact spot where my bra straps rest!

2] EXTRAS: I love when I open up a bag and find a smaller version of the bag stuffed inside.

3] PLENTY OF POCKETS: I'm a gadget girl. I love having little compartments for all my handhelds – cell, mints, camera, glasses, lip gloss, etc.

4] COOL COLOR: Although a girl can never have enough black bags, buy some bags with color. You will always get stopped for the "where did you find that?"

5] CONVERTIBLE: I always look for bags that have adjustable straps, which can zip/unzip to expand and or convert to a smaller version.

6] PRACTICAL: Go for function! I tend to be rough on my bags, so I look for bags I won't worry about ruining when it ends up on the floor.

Multi-purpose black bag
is a must have!

A tote in a neutral
color is a girl's go-
anywhere essential.

Wristlets, wallets, and coin purses
are perfect for keeping all your
smalls organized.

[RINGS & BLING]

Rings, bracelets, and bling things are a few of my favorite things — and are called EYE-CANDY for good reason. You see it and want to indulge in more and more. My stars love playing dress-up with fabulous accessories, and sometimes can't get enough. For this reason, I always have a supply of faux bling with me in a ziplock bag, so when the real gems have to go back after the photo shoot, I can give a celeb a little eye-candy to ease the loss. Some quickie tips: If you are going to wear rings — watch the salt — they may fit you as you are putting on the glitz and then be stuck-on-you, and may need some cocoa butter or mayonnaise to remove from your swollen finger...As for bracelets, keep in mind questions of activity and comfort. Will extra-chunky or dangly bracelets interrupt your writing on the computer? If you're at the beach, is the bracelet's metal potentially a painful heat-absorber...and/or will the salt water ruin delicate bling things

"TAKE CARE OF LUXURIES AND THE NECESSITIES WILL TAKE CARE OF THEMSELVES."

— DOROTHY PARKER

Scarves with a fringe are fun and casual, while a shiny one can work day to night!

[SCARVES]

Celebrities love a good scarf. It's perfect if you're running late for an audition or heading to that new dentist or meeting up with friends for dirty martinis. A good scarf will always add some "ooooomph!" – not to mention keep the chill off in the dental chair when the AC is pumped to the max. A scarf also comes in handy to throw over your hair if it's drizzling or if your hair is mischievously misbehaving. My celeb clients always keep a scarf in their IT bags. A fun way to wear a scarf is to first fold it in half – wrap the scarf around your neck – then make a knot with both ends. Another fun trick: Wrap the scarf around your neck backwards to forwards, and keep wrapping the scarf around your neck as many times as

[FASHION TAPE]

Many celebrities are known for undergoing secretive nips and tucks. But I'm not talking about plastic surgery. I'm talking about the nipping and tucking celebrities all do with the miracles of Fashion Tape! They use it to hold up strapless dresses, stop bra straps from slipping, amend puckering blouses, mend persnickety unraveling hemlines, prevent plunging necklines from becoming plunge-a-rama, and stop shoulder pads from drifting into becoming belly pads. **Basically, Fashion Tape is a double-stick treasure you can use on the double for any and all fashion emergencies.** It's faster than a speeding needle and smaller than a sewing machine – so you can always keep a package handily ready in your purse.

Change your perfume seasonally...light and fresh for summer – deep and musky for winter.

Keep a small vial of your favorite scent in your purse for emergencies!

[SCENTILATIONS]

We live in a visual world, putting emphasis on appearances. But if you smell like yesterday's sweat socks, it doesn't matter how you look. Slam-dunk a great impression by buttering yourself up with yummy smelling lotions and potions. Do NOT overdo too much of a good scent thing. If your hair conditioner or body lotion has a strong scent, cut back on perfume. Do NOT spray clothes and risk staining. Apply perfume on right and left side of your neck and/or inner wrists. These are you pulse points, so your scent will last longer. **Never rub wrists together after a spritz. It wears out the effect of the top layer of the perfume.** Consider mixing two different scents – to create a one-of-a-kind perfume. Choose one sweet scent (floral or vanilla) mixed with one citrusy (grapefruit or lemon). Breathstrips are a convenient way to keep minty fresh. They're flat enough to keep in your front pocket, without slipping out or bulging forward

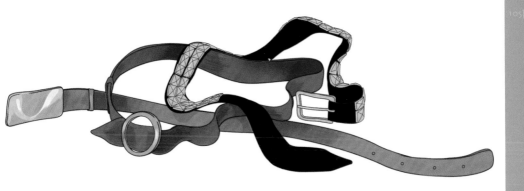

[BELTS]

A belt serves many purposes. Sometimes it's merely decorative. Sometimes it's a humilia-tion-saver. If your pants or skirt is baggy – definitely belt one on! **My favorite belt trick is buckling the belt at your hips instead of in the front, that way your tees lay flatter on your tummy.** A new belt will always make an old shirt or old dress look freshly fun! If you find an inexpensive belt you love that fits well, buy it in several colors. Try to choose belts which match your pants so you create an unbroken line. However you don't always have to match the belt to your shoes. If you wear a gold buckle you should wear gold, NOT silver, jewelry. If you're wearing an elastic waist, wear a pretty scarf as a belt. If your skirt or pants

[UNDERGARMENTOS]

Question: How many bras can a celeb have? Answer: As many drawers as she can fill. I like to organize bras by style rather than color, so if I am dressing a celeb for an event, I quickly know where to find the right bra for a spaghetti strap dress versus a backless dress. This prioritizing of style over color is helpful in all areas of the closet. Indeed, I have helped so many celebs redo their closets with this in mind, because everyone tends to put everything by color instead of style. **Here's another celeb behind-the-scenes-secret which is literally for the behind: Invest in Spanx!** They miraculously tuck you in – de-flawing any excess cushion in that tush. Suffice to say that every celeb in Hollywood has drawer fulls of this secret. Another must have: Cashmere socks! They keep feet toasty warm and are perfect to wear on a chilly airplane. A Hollywouldn't reminder: Never try to get away with navy, teal, or dark brown socks with black shoes! Someone will always notice! Make the effort to separate your socks according to style within small plastic boxes that fit inside your drawers. Later, if you're looking for knee-highs, they're all together and you will find those black ones you want in the style you want in that ASAP way that you want.

A Hollywouldn't reminder: Never try to get away with navy, teal, or dark brown socks with black shoes! Someone will always notice!

If you lose your glasses case, use a pretty (and clean!) sock. Once a week spritz a little Windex on dirty glasses.

[GLASSES]

Whether you're choosing glasses to protect you from the sun's evil rays or to help you see in full 20/20, always pick frames to match your face shape. For an Oval Face, choose frames which are as wide as (or wider than) the broadest part of your face. For a Base-Down Triangle Face, choose frames with color/detailing on the top half – and/or cat-eye frames. For Base-Up Triangle Face, choose frames which are wider at the bottom – and/or rimless. For a Square Face, choose narrow frames. Invest in gorgeous sunglasses to wear all year round – to protect your eyes and the delicate skin around them. If you're constantly on the computer, invest in tinted reading glasses to prevent eye strain. No matter what glasses you're wearing – or not wearing – always look for the beauty in yourself and others! Be happy!

" IF YOU GO as far as you can see, you will then see enough to go even farther. "

– JOHN WOODEN

acknowledgements:

To Karen – You expressed my words so incredibly well and came up with such stylish creative direction and packaging for this book – all of which SO represents who I am and how I feel.

Susie – You had me at hello.

Marcos – You are a creative genius.

Craig – Thanks for pushing it through.

Mom and Dad – Thanks for the all the pennies from heaven.

Neal – There you are...and so worth the wait. MLML.

Sydnee – Watching you reminds me I did my job.

Spencer – You inspire me every day with your vision.

Mindy – I am filled with pride to say you are my sister.

Dana – Your strength and determination never ceases to amaze me.

Aunt Sherry and Uncle Morrie – You stepped right in and never left.

Debbie and Rick – No words. Robert and David – Oy...life with a Hersh girl. Andrea – Wherever you go there I am. Reneé – You make it all good. Rochelle – My BFF Fashionista. Alison – You teach me by example. Barbara – Always there, no matter what. Jodi – Since we were five. Michael – You brought Karen and I together... who knew? LYMI. Ernie – No one listens better. Jeff – Thanks for your patience...always. Laurence and Olé – My biggest fans. Carlota – You made so much happen. Nini – I love you. Janis and Yvonne – My b-day sisters. Ariel – Very nice. Team Intuition – Couldn't be more grateful.

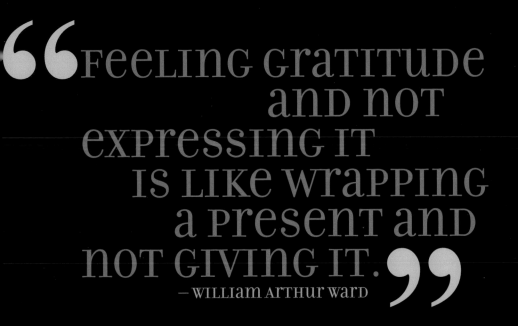

"FEELING GRATITUDE AND NOT EXPRESSING IT IS LIKE WRAPPING A PRESENT AND NOT GIVING IT."

— WILLIAM ARTHUR WARD

HOLLYWOOD INTUITION

[It's what separates fashion victims from fashion victors]

Published in the United States by powerHouse Books,
a division of powerHouse Cultural Entertainment, Inc.
37 Main Street, Brooklyn, NY 11201-1021
telephone 212 604 9074, fax 212 366 5247
e-mail: hollywoodintuition@powerHouseBooks.com
website: www.powerHouseBooks.com

First edition, 2009

Library of Congress Control Number: 2009928286

Hardcover ISBN 978-1-57687-526-1

Printing and binding by Transcontinental Printing G.P., Québec
Book Packaging/Creative Direction by Karen Salmansohn, www.notsalmon.com
Book design by Susie Mendive

A complete catalog of powerHouse Books and Limited Editions is available upon request;
please call, write, or visit our website.

10 9 8 7 6 5 4 3 2 1

Printed and bound in Canada